BEAT DEPRESSION
WITH SELF-HELP
TECHNIQUES

Best wishes

Andrew
Van

19/3/05

BEAT DEPRESSION WITH SELF-HELP TECHNIQUES

ANDREW VASS

APEX PUBLISHING LTD

First published in 2005 by
Apex Publishing Ltd
PO Box 7086, Clacton on Sea, Essex, CO15 5WN, England

www.apexpublishing.co.uk

British Library Cataloguing-in-Publication Data
A catalogue record for this book
is available from the British Library

ISBN 1-904444-25-3

Typeset in 11pt Baskerville by Maria Bright

Production Manager: Chris Cowlin

Cover Design Jenny Parrett

Printed and bound in Great Britain

PREFACE

Many writers have tried to convince people about the value of self-help techniques for coping effectively with depression. It would appear that they have often failed. Sometimes this is because the ideas and techniques they advocated have been either trivial or inadequate to the tasks of helping people with depression. Some books offer ideas and techniques, which are considered to be wrong by leading scientists.

Yet the need for self-help techniques seems undisputable. Newspapers are always reporting on celebrities who become depressed, lose confidence, or suddenly act in bizarre ways. Executives in business companies are reportedly suffering from anxiety or burn out. Many teenagers, suddenly facing the emotional roller-coaster rides of adulthood; with exam stress, relationship problems, career related difficulties, and drugs-induced - negative moods dragging them down, come close to being suicidal.

Yet the potential for self-help techniques to solve such problems is actually very good. There are some approaches to self-help, which are undoubtedly approved of by the scientists who investigate the empirical evidence of therapeutic outcomes. There are respectable writers who have written very useful and interesting books on self-help. Often, however, such books fail to combine the following qualities, which many readers need when they read such books. These are: Clarity, Brevity, Depth of Analysis, and Upbeat Interesting Writing. Another problem is that writers often adopt an ideological approach. This means they focus only on one approach to selp-help. Their enthusiasm for this one approach causes a great deal of time and space being invested in the theoretical basis for the idea. Their ideas may be great but the reader has lost sight of the trees, because the wood was too thick. This book in contrast, has the qualities I have referred to above. It is designed for people who want to improve their lives, escape from the tendency to suffer from depression, and generally become happy.

The book has adapted techniques from: Person Centred Therapy, Counselling, Cognitive Behavioural Therapy, Rational Emotive Behavioural Therapy, Hypnotherapy, Sport Therapy and Stoic Philosophy to help people to use Self-Counselling techniques for the treatment of depression. I think that list sounds interesting. For this reason, my book should be useful to school students, and young adults, as well as to middle aged and elderly people. A highly valued friend, Margaret Jarvie (a leading educational theorist and counsellor in Scotland) wrote:

"This is a book, which is long overdue as it provides guidelines for anyone with a concern for personal growth.
The advantages of having an identified framework and methodgy to apply to personal and social education is that it provides a structured approach which remains flexible. It is as a result of this, particularly appropriate in the context of personal and social education.
The points made in the context of Personal and Social education programmes are equally valid in situations that pertain between parents and their offspring as well as to individuals. One cannot help wondering if we would not create a better world to live, if all of us learnt and used the skills which this author sets to equip us with."

Margaret Jarvie, who has now sadly passed away, was an invaluable helper to me as I wrote this book. Her encouragemnet kept me on track. I acknowledge her contribution with my full respect.

My aim has been to demystify the Cognitive Therapies so that their usefulness is very clearly explained with interesting examples showing the benefits of Self-Help Therapy and the relevance of the theories of self-help treatments for depression. I hope that the success of this project will lead to the Cognitive Therapies becoming readily understood and used by both young and the old. In schools, homes, businesses, and libraries this book can be of value. It has both general relevance and specific value to mature people and many theatres of life.

What more do I need to say but read on and learn how to do Self-Counselling. This study could well transform your life.

- Andrew Vass, April 2004

CONTENTS

Chapter 1
Self-Counselling is Important

Task 1:Getting in touch with your inner world

When we go through a period of personal failure or a very upsetting time, we can either grow and develop through it or remain stuck in sad and depressing reactions. It has been found that if we suffer feelings of failure in childhood we may develop an inner discouraged layer, and then we hold on to this discouraged child part in our personality long into adulthood. This inner child part then tends to give us negative beliefs which confirm us in discouraged and anxious reactions when faced by future difficult events. So the learned sense of helplessness and discouragement makes us more easily depressed when we face new difficulties.

All through our lives such experiences occur, and all through our lives we are either growing or else being slowed down by negative reactions. We don't always recognise these negative reactions as being depressing. For example, feelings of sadness, anxiety or anger can be linked to depression, although this is not generally understood by the public at large. However, strong negative feelings all contribute to depressive thinking even when we don't feel we have become clearly depressed. We can, for example, become stuck with feelings of anger and not actually realise its depressing effects. The key to moving on from such difficult events is to achieve some kinds of resolution of the difficulties. But how can you get in touch properly with your inner world of feelings and thoughts so as to gain resolution? One way to do this is to become your own counsellor and understand the value of self-counselling.

Task 2: To understand self-counselling

Carl Rogers, the founder of person-centred therapy, inspired the development of the counselling approach. He believed that if you paid attention to surface feelings you could get in touch with deeper feelings. Just by spending time sensing your own experiences you could achieve fuller self-awareness[1]. It can be compared to peeling off the layers of an onion. Rogers believed that by studying feelings you could get to know your authentic self. This book is inspired partly by Carl Rogers, so I recommend that you try to investigate self-empathy which is the skill of attending to and exploring your own feelings (see glossary).

One way to do this is to write a dialogue with yourself. It is as if you are writing a play. Start with 'Me' and write something about a problem you are facing at the moment and how it makes you feel. Then write down 'C' (for counsellor) and try to suggest any feelings you may have and what the effects of them might be. Okay, see my example below of a young woman who was upset about having to leave the country she grew up in, and move nearer to her relatives.

GLOSSARY: Empathy
The technique of understanding feelings is called empathy. To use it fully, try to say to yourself, 'You feel ... because of ... and the effect is ...'
see example

Example of self-counselling technique

Me: I just don't feel positive about going to live abroad, and I know I should. I should feel positive because I will see more of my family. But Scotland is where I grew up, and I can't accept that I'm leaving it.

C: You feel very sad, because so much about Scotland really suited you. So the effect is that you find it difficult to feel at all positive about starting somewhere new.

Me: Yes, I should feel positive but I just feel moody about it and I'll feel my relatives are just strangers.

C: The situation feels uneasy for you, you seem to think that your natural anger about it will affect your relationships.

Me: Yes, it has plunged me into a sad and angry mood.

C: The bottom line is you have to work out what to do about your negative feelings before you are ready to move on and think about what's in it for you.

(Appendix 1 lets you see examples of techniques from counselling which we will explore later.)

You can see from this example that upset feelings were preventing this young woman from moving on and starting a new life. The self-counselling exercise, which just involved attending to her experiences, helped her to sense exactly how she was feeling. Notice that as well as having negative feelings she also suffered from having negative thoughts. Her negative thoughts were: 'I was happy in Scotland.', 'I can only be happy if I am in Scotland', 'I can't see myself being happy anywhere else' and 'How unfair it is for people to uproot me'. Some of these negative thoughts are particularly strong. They are conclusive and very negative. They are called 'hot thoughts'. We tend to express these thoughts in a vehement and emotional way.

Self-counselling is a way in which you can be fully in touch with sad feelings and thoughts about events and not simply deny their existence. To do self-counselling you have to become good at spotting your feelings and recognising their full effect. You will get further opportunities to consider how to become good at self-empathy in later chapters.

The exercise above involves acting like a professional interviewer and interviewing yourself. However, you can also investigate thoughts and feelings by using an arrow diagram. To do this you just have to write down something about a problem situation at the top of a page and then draw an arrow down the page. Perhaps you then could write down a feeling that the problem causes. Draw another arrow and write down a strong thought which you sense you have. Continue using the downward arrows to help you to explore your reactions to the problem. The important thing to realise here is that a willingness to examine your feelings is all you need right now. You don't have to be brilliant at it.

Hopefully, as you read this book you will find that using the techniques leads to more self-understanding, and therefore more choices for dealing with your feelings.

Question 1:   Can you recall the feelings and thoughts you had about an important event in your life? One example that is easy to work on is perhaps a holiday you went on at some time in your life. Either describe what it was like to a friend and your friend will try to spot how you felt, or write it in the self-counselling ways described above. Of course you might like to try working on a more difficult example. Remember, the aim is for you to get in touch with the kinds of feelings and thoughts that you had then.

Task 3: To see how to work on negative feelings

The young person in the example above had to try to work on her negative feelings and thoughts by checking out if there were other ways of looking at the situation. Is it possible that she could be happy going abroad because she would be able to go to a really good school? Perhaps she can think of various interesting cultural attractions about this foreign country with which she could get involved. Possibly she has met some of her cousins before and got on well with one of them. Basically, if she accepts the negative feelings and gives herself some space to explore and understand them fully, then she may be all the more able to think through alternative ways of viewing the situation.

According to cognitive therapists (who we will study in depth later), it is important first to understand fully how you feel and what your thoughts are. Only then can you see if there are alternative ways of looking at the situation. In my experience of being a counsellor, the example above is a common one. Having to move to a new country can trigger feelings of resentment and depression. However, if you are trying to work on the feelings, then the negative thoughts and deep sadness can be overcome, and with them the other very damaging reactions.

The example above also demonstrates a very common emotional

theme. For instance, when a person experiences a major failure in his/her life, it may affect him/her deep down in this very sad way. There probably is a sense of loss, humiliation and failure. There may be a change of job, or status or direction. However, the deep sadness controls his/her mind, making him/her dwell in the past and thus unable to see a way forward. Once again the person has to get in touch with the sad feelings and be aware of the aspects of his/her sad thinking. His/her conclusions about the situation matter. They are the upsetting thoughts and attitudes that need to be worked on before he/she can feel fully oriented towards his/her new way of life.

According to cognitive therapists, it is quite possible to be in touch with your feelings and at the same time try to see if you can figure out alternative ways of looking at the situation. For example, Mandy (a 25-year-old shop assistant) found herself becoming shy after repeated failures to meet up with pleasant lads of her own age. She was also having work-related problems at the same time. The whole situation became very discouraging and she found herself becoming a bit depressed. After trying to get in touch with her feelings and thoughts through self-counselling, she wrote down her most negative thoughts about the situation in her cognitive diary. Then she tried to consider which of these thoughts were her saddest ones, i.e. her most negative conclusions. Below is the excerpt from her diary. But, first read the glossary describing how a cognitive diary is used in self counselling.

GLOSSARY: Cognitive Diary
This exercise involves writing about a negative experience and the feelings caused by it. Then you list the negative thoughts that are linked to the experience. Try to suggest alternative ways of looking at items in the next column. Now, decide which are your strongest thoughts, your most negative conclusions and see if you can make a 'points for and against' table which can help you to debate the truth of these hot thoughts.

Cognitive diary

Thoughts	Alternatives
1. He did not enjoy chatting to me.	1. I don't know this.
2. He preferred to talk to Helen.	2. Boys are shy of girls they fancy.
3. I never get any luck.	3. No one gets luck all the time
4. I will have an appraisal at work and I am dreading it because I don't get on with one of my colleagues	4. But my boss has said that I am a good worker
5. I would like to apply for a management post, but I would make a fool of myself.	5. But perhaps I am quite highly regarded by my boss.

To do a cognitive diary, Mandy had to write a brief description of the situation. Then she had to write a column about her thoughts and a column showing alternative thoughts:

Mandy's hottest thoughts were 'I never get any luck' and 'My appraisal is bound to turn out bad.' She decided to make a table which examined the points for and against these claims. We will come back to examine her self-help exercises later.

Question 2:   Try doing a self-counselling exercise for yourself for a small problem you had some time ago. In the counsellor's dialogue try to spot all the kinds of feelings that the situation caused and try to identify the sad concluding thoughts. Then try to consider if there is a better way, and an alternative view you could have of the problem.

So, cognitive self-counselling is a helpful idea for people who wish to work on their tendency to get depressed. Firstly, the idea of being fully in touch with your feelings and upsetting thoughts is a sensible one. We often don't know exactly what is on our minds when we get upset about a difficulty. The more we can see the kinds of thoughts and feelings that affect us when we get upset, the more we can counter-act the negative thoughts. According to cognitive therapists, if we patiently work at reconsidering our negative thoughts we will regain control of our feelings. However, we do need to know a lot more about the kinds of thoughts that cause depressed feelings and that task will be the focus of the next few chapters of this book. The next chapter will help us to see clearly the effects of typical negative thoughts, and how they can be countered.

Revision + Key points from this chapter
*   When you face a personal difficulty, it is useful to get in touch with feelings and thoughts.
*   It doesn't matter how good you are at having 'self-empathy', the important thing is just to give yourself some space to do it. The minimum standard will be good enough.
*   By giving yourself 'space' to feel and experience your inner turmoil, you will find that you know yourself better. You sense the sad conclusions and hot thoughts and live authentically with your feelings..

*   Once you know what you are thinking and feeling you will become more able to use a cognitive thoughts diary, which involves writing down your thoughts and trying to reconsider them.

Chapter 2
Insights From Cognitive Behavioural Therapy

Task 1: To appreciate cognitive theories about the cause of upsets

According to cognitive therapists we often get upsets in life because we have a tendency to dwell on the sad aspects of life, we believe the worst, and we become pessimistic as a result. Our basic reaction is to jump to conclusions. Therefore, cognitive therapy is mainly about helping people to try to consider other ways of looking at situations.

Below are the key negative thought patterns identified by cognitive therapists. Notice that they are all similar in so far as they can all be called errors of judgement.

Why do we often need to work on our errors of judgement? Mainly because we tend to do 'all or nothing' thinking. This is when we see ourselves as either wonderful or worthless. We also see everything in black and white, and we get anxious that others will see us in the same negative light. We also tend to over-generalise. This tends to makes us expect bad luck because of one bad experience. Then we can get the dreaded 'mental filter'. This is when we seize a negative aspect of a situation and dwell on it. We also have a tendency to personalise things. This leads us into self-critical attitudes. In particular, it leads us to think in terms of 'shoulds' and 'musts'. It also means that if someone insults us we are inclined to maximise the meaning. We then tend to think that they meant to be really hurtful, and that the criticism is unbearably heavy. We often do 'mind reading' so that we assume we know what people are thinking of us despite the lack of evidence. 'Magnifying' is a common cause of anxiety. This is when we exaggerate the extent of a problem. Lastly, and worst of all is the 'catastrophizing' tendency. This is when we expect disaster to strike. We even fantasise about it happening and ask ourselves questions like, 'What if the worst happened?' We torture ourselves by allowing such thoughts to go round and round in our heads. *(See appendix 2 for full explanation of mental errors.)*

No wonder we have to keep on working on our natural tendencies to become defeatist, dissatisfied, anxious and depressed. It's because we can be defeatist. We very quickly come to believe the worst in difficult situations.

Task 2: To understand how the key negative thought patterns can be used in cognitive diaries.

Question 1:   Try to do a Self Counselling Dialogue for yourself and see if you can write up a cognitive diary with a thoughts analysis column. Remember to do the follow-up work that Mandy has outlined. This follow-up work involves looking at pros and cons relating to problem situations so that you can reconsider how realistic the negative thought is.

Also ask yourself 'Do things really need to turn out exactly as I expect?' When Mandy asked herself the question: 'How am I expecting things to turn out badly?', she found that she was most worried about how she would be treated by her line managers. She thought about how difficult it was for her to face appraisal inter-views in the past. She looked at evidence for and against the idea that such interviews would always be a cause of anxiety for her. She came to realise that her fearful attitudes were holding her back and preventing her from being happy when she found herself in the limelight.

Let us return to Mandy's ongoing experiment with self-counselling (see Chapter 1). Mandy has been trying to understand her own moodiness and tendency to be depressed. She has already done some work on her feelings of shyness with men. Now she is trying to consider if she should apply for a manager's post at her firm. She realises through doing self counselling that she is actually quite panic-stricken about the possibility of getting this job. She writes her thoughts in her cognitive diary. However, in the 'Alternative Thoughts' column she tries to use the key negative thought patterns to help her with her attempt to be more positive in her thinking.

Situation	Thoughts	Analysis of Thoughts
I will be given extra work and responsibility if I get promoted. I feel anxious.	1. The other workers don't respect my work.	1. This is an example of *mind reading*. I could do a *pros and cons* table on this so that I can check the evidence.
	2. I will feel worried that I will get into a mess, like I did the last time I was given responsibility.	2. This is *over-generalising*. Lightning seldom strikes twice in the same place.
	3. I get flustered when I'm under pressure, then my confidence goes down the tubes	3. This is very *black and white*. Look at the times when I was under pressure and do a *pros and cons* table of how I handled them
	4. At least I know what sales is like. I feel I don't know what management will be like, so I feel totally unready to take it on.	4. This is *magnifying*. I do know what managers do. I watch them do it every day.

	5. I will always be a failure and would be lucky to work in a low-paid job with no real status.	5. This *all or nothing thinking* just destroys my morale. There is no evidence around to tell me what the future holds. With lots of training courses available I could improve greatly.

Mandy's Appraisal

Mandy found that among her core negative beliefs was a tendency to be pessimistic and expect bad lack. She took a fresh look at her assumptions about how things would be bound to go wrong at her forthcoming appraisal. She wrote down pros and cons so that she could reconsider her assumptions. See example of balance sheet over page.

Notice how Mandy's balance sheet for her appraisal problems contains some of the typical cognitive thinking errors which I outlined earlier. The words 'here we go again' suggest that Mandy is jumping to conclusions. Can you find examples of 'Personalising' 'Magnifying' or 'Maximising the Meanings'?

Clearly folk like Mandy can get a lot of help from understanding cognitive therapy concepts and procedures. We will see more examples of cognitive therapy in later chapters.

Cons	Pros
* I just feel here we go again. I won't be given a proper hearing. Whatever I say I will be criticised. * Last time I ended up feeling guilty about not doing my job properly. * I hate it when people find things to criticise. * I know that some of the workers don't like me and my boss will be bound to take their side. They are all pals. * What if I get warned I could lose my job if I don't take on extra work or training courses. * I will probably agree to take on too much	* I may be commended for developing a good plan for self improvement. * If I am criticised for some things I may also be praised for other things. You have to take the bad with the good. * The Appraisal may help me to focus on exactly what I need to do to improve. So that will help me to prioritise on further training etc. * If my boss manages to take on board some of my concerns it may mean she understands things from my point of view much better. * No 'what if's'. there is no sign of a threat to my job.

Chapter 3
Why You Need Counselling
Techniques For Self-Counselling

Task 1: To consider how far techniques used in counselling interviews are useful for self-counselling

When I operate in a counselling role I tend to use the following techniques. We will develop our understanding of them throughout this book, and also think about how far they might be useful for self-counselling. At the very first meeting I have with a client I begin with a technique called a door opener. This is when you show that you recognise the nature of the problem the client is trying to outline and ask him/her to tell you more about it. Then I move on to reflection of content and reflection of feelings (often termed empathy) This empathy dialogue helps the client to explore the inner world of his feelings and emotional reasoning. I may eventually use a minimum encourager or an open-ended question to encourage the client to talk further about aspects of the problem. A minimum encourager is like asking a question. You take a key word or phrase that the client has used and refer it back to the client in a questioning way. So how do these techniques get put together in a counselling interview? See my example below of a 35-year-old man called William who has come to talk about the difficulties he has with his four-year-old son.

Example of counselling interview

William: I am so glad you could see me counsellor. I feel I just have to talk to someone about my little boy. He gets up at night every night and he makes a terrible noise with his toys and he wakes my wife and I up and it's most tiring for us both.

Counsellor: Small children can be quite a cause of stress, so I'm very glad to sit down and talk about how things are going for you. Could you tell me some more about what's been happening? *(door opener)*

William: Well, John just seems to be so destructive and attention seeking when he gets up at night and it just wears us out and we get stressed and irritated.

Counsellor: So the first thing you want to explore is the way that he seems to cause problems at night. *(reflection of content)*

William: Yes. Somehow or other he manages to get us both to be quite neurotic, and then I get anxious about what's the right way to handle him.

Counsellor: You're puzzled about how you and your wife get into a state about things. You feel anxiety about how things are going. *(empathy)*

William: Yes. Things just seem to get out of hand. We get so angry at him. When he starts banging with his hammer on the radiator his mum just gets so fed up she threatens to leave. She starts packing her bags, and I'm saying, 'Look, calm down! calm down!!'

Counsellor: You get worried and think, 'It's a nightmare'. *(empathy)*

William: Yes it makes me think things are hopeless and then wee John is also really angry and frightened. And I think, 'This can't be good for him'.

Counsellor: You feel really sad for John but you also think that you are stuck with no adequate solution. Do you have any ideas about what has caused the problem to start and reach this level of frustration? *(open-ended question)*

Question 1: How is this empathy dialogue helpful? To what extent are these techniques of Counselling useful for self-counselling?

I have decided to give you some help with this question. So consider the points below.

* Notice the variety of feeling words used by the counsellor.
* Words like 'you feel puzzled' help the client to be self-aware.
* The client is being helped to stay in touch with both his feelings and his negative conclusions which operate at a feeling level.
* The open-ended question partly strays from feelings but it invites the client to say more about what's on his mind about the problem, for example how far he thinks himself and his wife are to blame.

GLOSSARY: Open ended questions

There are closed questions and open-ended questions in counselling. A closed question asks for a fact, like 'What is your job?' An open question asks about an aspect of a situation. For example, you could ask a client 'How are things going for you at work right now?'

To make really good use of open-ended questions, it might be useful to compare counselling to a dramatic production. Let us imagine that you arrived very late to see a play. It is now the break and you have the good fortune to meet the lead character and ask him about the story. You might like to know: What has been the main development? How did it come about? What is the lead character supposed to feel about it? How does he feel right now? What are the other aspects of the plot? The main characters? The jobs they all do? Their relationships?

Question 2.: Using the drama production comparison above, write down some examples of good open-ended questions that could be used in counselling.

Question 3: Is this example a good one for any person who wants some training in cognitive counselling or mentoring?

Imagine that you are role-playing the situation. John has brought his son with him to see the counsellor. Either try to do the role-play with a friend or just use a chair and play both parts so that you sit on the other chair when you act out the counsellor's role.

How do people like John and Mandy get real benefits from cognitive counselling? Here is a list of the main counselling techniques which help. See if you are familiar with any of them from any counselling training courses you have been on:

* Door opener;
* Show empathy;
* Rationales;
* Concreteness search;
* Additive empathy;
* Challenge;
* Reflect content;
* Open questions;
* Paraphrases;
* Minimum encourager;
* Summaries;
* Chaining; and
* Action plans.

(See appendix 1 for a full explanation of these terms.)

Later in this chapter, I will show how clients benefit from the use of these varied techniques. Then you will be much more aware of how to do cognitive counselling either in self-counselling or in co-counselling.

By the way, if you do not like the idea of written self-counselling exercises it is possible to use the arrow diagram technique I outlined in the first chapter. When your problem seems fairly straightforward (as in Mandy's case which we saw earlier), you can move quickly into using the cognitive diary or an ABC. Form (which you will come across in later chapters). In William's case the problem may not be straightforward so it needs to be explored. Only then can the counsellor gain a concrete understanding of what is going on.

More counselling techniques for self-counselling
Task 2: To look at the uses made of concreteness search
Concreteness search is when you:
*   try to understand problems more concretely;
*   look for specific negative thoughts as in a cognitive thoughts diary; and
*   consider which aspects of problems need to worked on first.

Let's get back to our client William. He was asked an open question about how the problem seems to have developed. After his response to this question, the counsellor helped him to weigh up the significance of what he had said by summarising aspects of it and having a mind map made, showing key parts. Look at the mind map below and see how it helped him to reach a conclusion about these areas that he might need to work on. Now that various problems have been outlined, the counsellor and client have to sort out which one they would like to work on first. It can be useful to pick an immediate problem, one that the client feels strongly about at the time of the interview. You will see in task 3 which problem the client chose to work on first.

Five years ago we lost baby William due to cot death.

Perhaps my wife and I are both often up-tight and anxious about how we handle a child.

Mind-map of William's Problems

Perhaps it's me to blame. I become so nervous and I tell myself some negative things like 'I'm a bad father', 'We are bad for John', 'He will grow up having mental health problems'.

Did this event affect our marital relationship? I am certainly aware of how I tend to nag and be intolerant at times.

My wife became a strong church-goer after baby William died, but I don't really like her church. It is too narrow and uncaring for me.

Right now this is making me moody and probably it is making me handle her unsympathetically.

Task 3: To understand how challenge is used in cognitive counselling.

Challenge involves:
* using paraphrases to focus on the precise nature of the negative thoughts;
* then asking a key question that could make the client think about whether the negative thought is correct or incorrect; and
* possibly inviting the client to think out better ways of looking at the situation using a cognitive diary or an ABC form.

Let's take a look at an example of the use of challenge. On William's mind map, he had referred to an immediate problem that was making him moody with his wife. He had taken a dislike to the narrow and uncaring attitudes that he felt were exhibited by the church they both attended. See how the counsellor challenges his negative conclusions in the excerpt below.

William: Yes, I am annoyed about the church situation and I feel my feelings are simply repressed and just disconfirmed by other people.

Counsellor: You feel frustrated because of what you see to be narrow attitudes and the effect it has on you; it 'puts down' your more liberal views. (empathy)

William: Yes, I tend to think their macho gung-ho use of God's wrath to condemn all non-attenders to be primitive and insensitive.

Counsellor: Primitive? (minimum encourager)

William: Yes, it's like they are saying, 'Here I go again getting control. Mind over matter; we mind and you don't matter'

Counsellor: So you see it as narrow and uncaring. (paraphrase)

William: Yes, it's narrow and uncaring. It's like saying, 'Here's Christianity. It's how we see it. You punters should take it our way.

You don't have to reason for yourselves.

Counsellor: *Is the evidence you have good evidence of insensitivity?*
(challenge)

William: *Yes and no. For example, they are extremely kind. And perhaps I read too much into how their behaviours all add up to the same kind of thing.*

Counsellor: *Perhaps you are beginning to think that their behaviours are narrow but not uncaring and that you sometimes get drawn into a bit of mind reading. Is that perhaps correct?*
(challenge)

GLOSSARY: Paraphrases

Paraphrases are brief summaries that reflect the client's thinking. Paraphrases correctly mirror the sad conclusions that the client seems to be making. This attending to the client's extreme thoughts is every bit as important as attending to his feelings.

Notice that just one question which asks a client, 'How good is the evidence?' can prove to be vitally useful to helping a client to work on their feelings. In later chapters we will see more examples of how William's problems can be worked on using the cognitive therapies, and you will see that the lessons on how to manage grief, nervousness and intolerance can be applied to your own life, and so help you to overcome depression.

To conclude this section on counselling techniques consider again the important role played by open-ended questions. From the first door opener, eg the open-ended question, 'Could you tell me more about your problem?', we saw that open-ended questions helped the client to talk. The counsellor then simply attended to the client's narration of concerns, feelings and thoughts. The later use of open-ended questions invited the client to look at aspects of his problem situation more fully and then later on to look at a specific example of the situation. Clearly the open-ended question technique provided the hinge on which the whole process of counselling opened out. For those of you trying to study the significance of these examples of counselling for the purposes of self-counselling, let me create a useful analogy. Open-ended questions are like a mouse for a computer. You want to use the mouse to investigate the icons on your screen. An open-ended question takes you to the icon; empathy and paraphrases take you inside the icon so that you allow its' contents to be manifested. So perhaps this chapter has shown you that good techniques for self-counselling interviews - which include the use of open-ended questions and mind maps - may be helpful for improving your ability to work on negative feelings. Clearly to do self-counselling effectively you need to have a basic understanding of counselling techniques and counselling theories, and also knowledge of the various self-help exercises that are available. We will deal with these in more depth in the next few chapters.

Chapter 4
Next Step -
Comparing the Cognitive Therapies

This book will utilise concrete topics to build up a clear understanding of the usefulness of the cognitive therapies. The two main cognitive therapies are called cognitive behavioural therapy and rational emotive behavioural therapy.

Cognitive behavioural therapy was developed in university psychology departments in the 1970s. Its methodology and effectiveness has therefore been empirically assessed. Nowadays it is considered to be the main treatment for depression. Its theoretical basis is partly developed from behaviourism, and partly from rational emotive behavioural therapy, which was formulated by several leading American psychiatrists in the 1950s.

The key idea in cognitive theorising is that errors in thinking play a significant part in causing negative states of mind, and inappropriate behaviours. Below are some typical thinking errors:

* All or nothing thinking - This makes you view yourself and others as either wonderful or worthless. Your thinking is very much black and white, i.e. good and bad, with no shades of grey.
* Over-generalisation - This links into a pessimistic sense that you will get bad luck in your life. One bad experience proves you can't trust luck, other people, or life.
* Personalisation - This may promote guilt, shame or defensiveness, and denial. This thinking focuses on the blame that could be landed on oneself. It's as if one sees oneself as the centre of the universe.
* Mental-filter - you seize a negative aspect of a situation and dwell on it.
* Jumping to conclusions - You make assumptions (this is termed

'fortune telling') and you draw conclusions from non-verbal evidence (termed 'mind reading').

So the lesson from the cognitive therapies is that when people get depressed they tend to develop mental errors which cause strong negative emotions and discouragement - in other words the basic ingredients of depression.

So how do you work on the mental errors that underlie negative emotions? You look for feelings and the precise thoughts that relate to them. You find the errors and debate them. The client almost magically begins to come to terms with the upsets.

Well, the achievement does look like very clever conjuring - in actual fact the achievement is not easy! Client and counsellor both use skills to overcome the problems. The important thing to realise here is that if you thought that changing negative feelings was easy to do you would become insensitive. You would fail to have emotional intelligence. You would not take your own emotional reactions or people's emotional reactions very seriously.

Now, I stated earlier that cognitive behavioural therapy (CBT), which was developed in the scientific establishments, is nowadays seen as the more respectable of the sister therapies. However, I sometimes still prefer rational emotive behavioural therapy (REBT) because its basic theory is also valuable. [2]Ellis, the leading writer on REBT, saw the essential nature of these mental errors in a different way. He viewed them as being too global, too definitional, in that they involve defining self, life, or others, as being awful. Look back again at the first three cognitive thinking errors above and notice that they amount to defining self as awful. Therefore, when in rational emotive theory, a client is said to be 'awfulising', it means that he is seeing something as 100% bad. This is about more than just making faulty assumptions. Emotions, thoughts and negative images seem to be working like a propaganda network in which they reinforce one another in coming to these negative verdicts that REBT has termed 'awfulising'. From this theoretical perspective, REBT places greater emphasis on the importance of 'exercises' for self-help than does CBT. This is because the use of debate may not be sufficient to help a client to break out of the propaganda of his/her 'emotional reasoning'. He/she may need to use several exercises involving disputing, debating and imagining techniques in order for him/her to break out of his/her negative state. Now, if debating and disputing showed the client that his/her negative rating (or 'awfulising') was a mental error, then the client's negative feelings could be changed. Ellis saw that people needed an appropriate philosophy as well, one that would help them to be more rational about their problems. This more appropriate philosophy could be taught through the use of 'bibliotherapy', whereby the client will benefit just by reading about ideas that can help him/her to be rational. Several of the later chapters of this book can be termed 'bibliotherapy'. In REBT the word rational means to:

* think logically about problems;
* take a moderate view of self and the world - an enlightened view that is derived from philosophy;
* think out solutions to problems that do not end up just becoming self-defeating. This means that you do not want to have solutions that work well for you today but give very bad results tomorrow;
* think ethically about solutions. Ethical solutions will neither be self-defeating nor will they do damage to other people.

Thus, REBT leans more towards the idea that good therapy firstly involves highlighting thoughts relating to the awfulness of problem situations; then secondly you debate, dispute and teach a more appropriate philosophy. CBT looks more generally at mental processes and focuses on correcting the mistaken assumptions. In reality, both therapies are similar and the leading therapists have no major disagreements about the value of their procedures. REBT may look easier for the beginner because the use of ABC exercises for self-counselling engenders concrete and well-structured activities (as you will see in the next few chapters). Bibliotherapy is also easy for the beginner to utilise and I hope you enjoy reading my attempts at bibliotherapy as I try to explain why REBT theory has been very helpful to me and my family. These therapies clearly complement each other. For this reason they have been collectively called 'the cognitive therapies'. In this book I have set out to demystify the cognitive therapies, and show how they can be useful for self-counselling for depression.

Chapter 5
Victims of Bullying and Understanding Depressive Experiences

Task 1: To consider the nature of depressed states

In the past I have been successful at helping school students who suffered from bullying. I have found that the kinds of feeling and thoughts that such victims have are very similar. Sometimes students are able to tell you how they are feeling. From this you can help them to work out their upsetting thoughts. At other times students seem more aware of their thoughts and attitudes. Again, from this you can help them to work out how they are feeling.

Victims of bullying exhibit feelings that seem depressive in the following respects. Firstly, they appear to be down and pessimistic about coping with their difficulties. I tend to use the REBT approach to

A: Activating Event	B: Thoughts	C: Feelings
Bullied in school	1. I hate it when friends see me being slagged. I don't expect my friends to like me. 2. I feel so sad about the fact they are calling me names 3. I get angry with the bullies but then they threaten to hit me again 4. Teachers can't help 5. I am too ashamed to talk about it. I feel like a fool	Angry, sad, embarrassed, frightened, helpless, discouraged

help such people because I like the ABC format, (and I will explore its value throughout this chapter). Also, I normally use disputing techniques to help these victims of bullying. The ABC form shows the typical combination of feelings and thoughts that a victim of bullying tends to have. (See previous page for exercise).

Now, in order to use REBT to help such a person you have to use arguments and disputes that focus on changing the discouraged thinking and the very sad attitude. Move now to D - Debate and Disputes column and deal with each thought in column B so you argue that a better way of looking at things is possible. I started on point 5 as it seemed the easiest thought to argue against.

D: Debate
5. A person can act foolishly or seem foolish yet not be a fool. The only foolish thing you are doing is losing your calmness because that stops you telling the teacher.
1. If this happened to your best friend wouldn't you feel sympathetic? So it is not correct to think that your friends must dislike you.
2. Don't tell yourself how sad it is. That doesn't help.In life we have to learn how to walk tightropes and people do learn how to do this.
3. So anger isn't helping either. It's black and white to see them as bad people. Then you feel beaten and you forget a major rule for living which is 'we all live with some risk - each day we cross roads'.
4. Let's calmly calculate the risks and the benefits of a teacher helping. With these improved thoughts you can walk the tight-ropes of your life.

Question 1:   Look back at the ABC form for the victim of bullying. Can you tell exactly which thoughts correspond with each feeling?

Concreteness search using the ABC form with William

Counsellor: William, in the mind map we looked at earlier, we thought out some important things for you to work on. One item from the list was the way both yourself and your wife become uptight about how you handle your child. Is it okay for us to spend some time on this problem right now? (OPEN ENDED QUESTION)

William: Yes, go ahead.

Counsellor: Now, I want to use an ABC form to work on this because I think some of your feelings and thoughts are not very accessible to you. The ABC form helps me to work out the thoughts you must have in order to account for why you have several upsetting feelings. (giving a rationale)

The counsellor now develops the ABC form with William. It ends up looking like the one which follows:

A: Activating Event	B: Awful Beliefs	C: Consequence
The situation of trying to get John to behave appropriately.	1. I don't like it when I am having to deal with difficult situations. 2. Having children is unrewarding. I've already had a sad bereavement. 3. My wife should be good at it.	Upset, nervous, discouraged, angry, sad, anxious about how to handle the situation.

The counsellor now returns to the discussion of the problem.

Counsellor: William, as I expected, the negative thoughts you have reported do not entirely account for the strong negative feelings you have explored with me. For example, let's take the thought 'I don't like it when I am having to deal with difficult situations'. Would that thought, which just reflects on your likes and dislikes, actually account for your feeling upset, discouraged and angry? So, instead of the words 'like' or 'dislike' could we consider what you actually must be saying to yourself to account for your strong feelings? (concreteness search)

William: *I think I am saying , 'It's hard and it shouldn't be that hard'.*

Counsellor: Okay, and similarly could we consider what you are actually saying to yourself in the last point about your wife.

William: *I think I am saying, 'This should be women's work. Women should be good at it.*

Counsellor: And if they are not? (chaining)

29

William: *I suppose it shows a failure of character. It's like I can't see any excuse for it.*

Counsellor: *Is that perhaps a little extreme William? (challenge)*

Notice how the Counsellor used the ABC form and a challenge question to help William to reconsider his problems. A technique called chaining was also used in this dialogue.

GLOSSARY: Chaining

Chaining is so called because by asking the question 'why?' repeatedly you go down a chain until you get to the real answer. For example, the counsellor might ask a client, 'Why would it be so awful if your daughter burst into tears?' The response is, 'It would make me feel like a bad mother'. The counsellor then enquires, 'Why would it be awful to have this feeling of being a bad mother?' The response is 'because my husband used to tell the kids that mummy's a bad mother. The day he left us two years ago he said to Janet, "Make sure mummy behaves well". His attitude has put a huge strain on my relationship with the children. 'So what did that make you feel about yourself?' I felt more like the naughty daughter than the parent of this family.

So chaining can help a counsellor to find out exactly how a client feels depressed and discouraged. When clients discover through the chaining process that their self-concepts or views of others are a little too negative, they are quite willing to try to move on from the depressing conclusions. In the situation above, the conclusion, 'I am a bad mother' is obviously quite extreme. These extreme views can be called 'personal meanings' or 'core negative beliefs'. Some cognitive therapists claim that people can develop core negative beliefs from childhood and still be affected by them long into adult life. The examples of Mandy's problems in chapter 2 bear out this idea. Her self-concept, self-esteem and expectations of life were all very negative but were successfully worked on with cognitive therapy.

Task 2: Additive empathy helps you become more aware of your depressed state

A teacher had just been promoted to a counselling role in a big school. He felt quite overwhelmed by the difficulties of his new job. He decided he had to go on a summer training course on counselling at a local college. While on that course he did a self counselling (SC) exercise. In this exercise the skill of additive empathy proved to be most useful.

> **GLOSSARY: Additive Empathy**
> This is when you use empathy to explore feelings and problems. While you benefit from staying in your negative mood by becoming more self-aware, you also explore your feelings by seeing the implications and by making deductions. This self-exploration is called additive empathy. While doing it you may find yourself exploring an aspect of your problem that previously had been overlooked. You may sense the different feelings - depression, sadness, anger, etc., more fully.

Mike: I have really enjoyed this counselling course, and I have learned a lot, but somehow I feel dissatisfied about how things are going.

SC: You have very positive feelings and a lot of satisfaction in what you have done. But, on the other hand, you have a vague negative doubt. (empathy)

Mike: Yes, the course itself was totally positive and I have no regrets about it.

SC: So, when you say, 'how things are going' are you perhaps talking generally? (additive empathy)

Mike: Yes, perhaps I have some concerns about how my wife and children are getting on.

S.Cou: So while you have been on this course, you perhaps have not had time to think about them. (additive empathy)

Mike: *I'm sure it sounds terrible, but I just feel I'm not doing things right at home.*

SC: *You are not feeling entirely comfortable about the situation at home. (empathy)*

Mike: *Yes, it's like I'm not feeling too happy with myself. It's like I've been so occupied that I've neglected them. I've made no plans for the holidays, and I'm quite wrapped up in this course.*

SC: *It's like there is an impasse and you can't quite cross over it. You have been course centred, and very preoccupied and that feels disappointing for you to have to admit it. (additive empathy)*

Mike: *That's right, but you know I can perhaps get to grips with this. It's time for me to throw out the stuffy books, get into light-hearted mode, and start planning a holiday. My family have coped with me on a course and they deserve to be well rewarded.*

Once again you can see that the skills of attending to negative feelings and thoughts can help greatly. Once Mike became immersed in the exploration of his negative feelings, he found that it became possible for him to reconsider his attitudes and move on with an enthusiastic and more appropriate attitude.

You may like the idea of doing self-counselling by using the interview technique. On the other hand, you may feel that the cognitive thoughts diary or the ABC form look easier to work with. If you experiment with the different types of self-help exercises described in this book, you will eventually find that you can benefit from using each of them to suit your needs in the different situations that require self counselling.

However, even if you don't become a regular user of self-help exercises, the book will still have helped you to develop an ability to think more rationally. The concept of being 'rational' comes from rational emotive theory. To be rational is to be logical and think clearly in ways that help you to accept that you can cope with some risk in life while not becoming frustrated or depressed when facing difficulties. Being rational involves having good self-acceptance even when you do sometimes mess up. Being rational also involves thinking clearly about future goals and not accepting solutions to life-problems which become self-defeating in the long run. There is no advantage to you from doing things that get good results today but lead to terrible results tomorrow. So being rational is about thinking logically and calmly about events and also not being self-defeating.

Question 3:   What did you learn from the Self Counselling example above about the skills of Additive Empathy?

So in this chapter we have seen how ABC forms can help with depression. The examples above have shown us that when people develop sad, negative thoughts, these thoughts become far more discouraging and morale-sapping than they realise. For this reason, ABC forms, chaining and additive empathy can help us to see more deeply into how a situation is making us feel. Angry thoughts and frightening thoughts can also be depressing. For this reason we have to turn our attention to morale, anger and fear as issues that have to be considered within the context of depression.

Chapter 6
Improve Your Morale

Some people wonder what are the skills of having good morale. I do not aim to give this question exhaustive coverage here, but I would like to show how, by attempting to think in more logical ways, you could achieve much better morale.

How important is good morale for being a good friend? Well, imagine that you are a school student and you and your best friend have auditioned for the leading role in a drama production. Sadly, you did not get the part but your friend did. Yes, your morale might suffer because of this. And yes, you might be envious or annoyed at your best friend.

According to cognitive therapists, the reason people can experience morale problems in such situations is because they see things in black and white and don't manage to consider alternative ways of looking at the situation. In particular, they tend to think either 'I'm on top' or 'I'm a flop'.

REBT brings two further theoretical considerations to help explain morale problems. People have a tendency to deal in 'awfuls' i.e. their thinking and feeling slip into 'This is awful' mode or 'Life is awful' or 'I am awful' - 1=0 as a result of this.

So one very important logical idea that a person should hold on to in a morale-sapping situation like the drama production catastrophe outlined above, is, 'When I am not on top I am not a flop'. An alternative way of looking at the crisis is to say to oneself, 'Never mind if I only get a small part. I could still be the best small-part person in town!' There are professional actors out there who make a mint out of being small-part actors.

Finally, think how good it is for your character to change the 'life is awful' verdict that we humans often suffer from. In this case the 'life is awful' verdict is a kind of demand that things be especially fair for you.

REBT teaches us that there are no laws of the universe promising that life will be good and fair to us. The universe is a cold bleak kind of place. It doesn't care about you or me! So it would be better for you to adopt a stoical philosophy, which can help you to live with things if they can't be changed.

A very good way of helping oneself to escape from the demanding mood is to try actively to feel pleased for other people when they succeed and always be keen to play any support role that helps to further the group success or community success. This attitude really helps you to enjoy being a small-part player. It also justifies the idea that being a small-part player is good for you. It goes hand in hand with the value of wanting to contribute to the success of your group and community.

This attitude also helps you to cultivate other qualities that are considered valuable in friendship, such as being non-possessive, non-demanding and non-egotistical, being sincere and genuine. Now I wonder if you know exactly what these terms mean? The last part of Chapter 7 on being a good friend will help you to explore these terms.

Let us turn our attention to a final way in which a fall in morale can be seen to interfere with your friendship skills. Once again, we will see that a more logical way of looking at the problem helps to overcome the difficulty.

Imagine that in some way your friend has embarrassed you. Perhaps he/she has said something about you or has said something really silly that reflected on you. Of course to help yourself with the anger you feel you will need to remember the logical idea I outlined earlier about there being no laws of the universe to guarantee you an easy life. But the new problem that is central to this is embarrassment.

Embarrassment is, of course, a huge cause of human misery and deserves our full attention. When young men sit silently alongside desirable members of the opposite sex or when they chat away in a nervous and not very interesting way, it is because they fear embarrassment. After attempting to invite out 'a pretty young thing', a young man's morale may collapse because she has turned him down. Again, he feels that the whole affair has ended in public embarrassment and humiliation.

A key logical idea to remember about embarrassment is as follows: 'Anything embarrassing that happens to you is only a ten-day wonder. Yes, this means it will be forgotten about by all and sundry in just ten days! That's right, exactly ten days - no more, no less; according to the old saying!'

If a logical idea like that helps you to be a 'shame attacker', i.e. a person who forcefully and vigorously tries to refuse to be embarrassed when struck by the blows of life, then you will find that you are practising utilising skills that will enable you to be more relaxed when with friends, more fun to be with and more open to trying out new and interesting activities in your life.

Lastly, your increased awareness about how all of us can suffer from blows to morale and embarrassment can make you a more considerate, respecting kind of person.

Once again, we can see that the writers of the rational emotive and cognitive theories did have an interesting angle on life. If we can work on the thoughts that underlie our feelings and make ourselves more logical, we can cope better with life and do better. These two therapies do combine well to help us to work on depressed tendencies. In chapters 8-10 I will examine how rational emotive therapies help people to work on the global, definitive, self-labels that undermine confidence and therefore contribute to discouragement.

Chapter 7
Being a Good Friend

Being non-possessive, non-defensive and non-demanding

* To be non-possessive means that you don't try to control your friends and run their lives.
* To be non-defensive means that if criticised you don't simply argue in a way that is solely about defending yourself at all costs.
* To be non-demanding means that you don't get angry all the time and make demands about what other people should do for you.

These qualities are considered to be ones that help people to relate well to others. If you read the last chapter again, relating to applying philosophy to morale problems, you will see that the ideas in it help you to cultivate these qualities.

However, we should be careful to consider exactly what these concepts do and don't really mean. Being non-possessive:

* does not mean that you should never ask a person to do something *with* you; and
* does not mean that you should never ask someone to do something *for* you.

The key criterion here is that you accept how they feel if they don't want to fit in with your needs.

Being non-possessive and non-demanding helps you to cope with the unexpected. For example, you may be able to accept that the male way of reacting to events is sometimes very different from the female way. Therefore you should try to be aware of the differences and make allowances for individual characteristics. Below is an example of just such a problem taken from a book by Gottman, Why Marriages Succeed Or Fail:[3]

'In the movie Terms of Endearment a scene between Aurora and

37

Garrett illustrates the mutual discomfort produced by women's desire to express emotion and men's tendency to avoid it ... Aurora has just told Garrett that she loves him. He hasn't responded so she asks him if he's had any reaction to her avowal of love. Not realising how difficult it might be for her to ask him this question, Garrett jokes back, saying 'I don't know what to say, except my stock answer.' Aurora asks him what this might be. He replies, 'I love you too kid' - an answer that hurt her, because it's a stock answer rather than a heartfelt feeling for her.'

According to cognitive therapists, we often suffer in life because we quickly jump to conclusions. You can see that the example above is a very good one for really showing how significant this problem can be.

My concluding point here is that, as you try to cultivate the qualities that we have considered in this chapter, you will find yourself being better able to cope with friends and the unexpected things that can happen when you are cultivating friendship. Your morale will also become better as you cultivate values that help you to feel good about yourself even when you are not on top. Now that we have worked on the values that underlie REBT, we will turn to examine more closely the concepts that rational emotive therapists employ. You will see that they are similar to the cognitive therapy ones and, because they are similar, you will not find the experience of studying them too complicated.

Chapter 8
Can Confidence be Learned?

Task1: To consider the causes of lack of confidence

At any age there are lots of difficult tasks that have to be dealt with. As these tasks are difficult, it is quite natural that we all feel unconfident about doing them.

To understand why difficult situations cause a lack of confidence, you have to study 'awfulising'. This is a word from REBT, which refers to the way we tend to overstate how awful things are.

Example

Imagine that you had been stood up last night. This can be represented in an ABC form:

A: the activating event

B: the awful beliefs you have about the event.

C: the consequence, e.g. feelings you then get.

A: **Activating event**

      I was stood up last night.

B: **Beliefs**

      1. This is awful. He seems a really super person.

      2. He couldn't really have liked me at all.

      3. I've just made a fool of myself.

      4. Everyone will be looking at me in the Geography class.

C: **Consequences**

      I feel upset, embarrassed, hurt, humiliated and unconfident.

You could say that we are all like a Leaning Tower of Pisa:

    *   Our confidence can be knocked;

    *   Our morale can completely cave in;

* We can't cope with embarrassment; and
* We sometimes give ourselves self-caricatures - 'I looked a real fool'.

Question 1:   Can you make a Leaning Tower of Pisa diagram. Round your drawing of a leaning tower write examples of the way your confidence has been knocked in the past.

Task 2: The solution to confidence - get out of your whirlpool

To overcome the lack of confidence tendency you just need to get out of your whirlpool. A whirlpool is a negative mental state in which you just torture yourself with 'I-obsessions'. 'I-obsessions' involve thinking:
* I should do better in life.
* I must be a success.
* I was a complete and total failure.
* I rate as useless and I = 0.
* Life is awful.
* Therefore this kind of problem is too big for me to face.

Example 1

Let me give you an example of a young man suffering a whirlpool effect. He was a pop singer and songwriter. One day he was asked to play in a pub. It seemed a big step up for him - he would actually get paid. Instead of being happy, he became very nervous. His thoughts were:
* 'This is too big for me'
* 'I must do my best or there will be no excuse for me.'
* 'I could let everyone down badly.'
* 'The punters will notice any mistake I make.'

The motto he learned was:

Instead of emphasising the 'I-ness' of what
you are doing emphasise the 'it-ness'

What does that mean? Could that motto work for you?

Example 2

Another example of 'I-obsessions' is that of a university student who found that university can become really stressful. His thoughts were:
* 'I must do well.'
* 'I can't be happy with myself if I fail.'
* 'My parents will be so disappointed if I fail.'

He learned to keep in mind the mottos below:

I = A lot more than just my achievements

Is this true? Do we all = a lot more than just our achievements? and

I am lots of

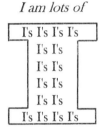

The basic truth is that to get out of whirlpools you need to change your 'musts' and 'shoulds' into preferences. This helps you to make your self-image less global and less negative. For example, 'I prefer to be a success', not 'I must', and not 'I've got to at all costs'.

Example 3

A lady had been having a mental breakdown because she was not very good at her job. Her therapist helped her by pointing out to her that:
* Her way of feeling sorry all the time was her sickness
* She was emphasising the 'I-ness' of what she was doing instead of the 'it-ness'.
* Making some mistakes now and again does not justify a person getting the sack.
* Failing in some things is not the same as being a failure.

Question 2: Take a few examples of the problems you wrote on your Leaning Tower diagram and see if you have any 'I-obsessions' concerning them. Make a drawing of a whirlpool and write around the drawing examples of your 'I-obsessions'.

Question 3: Write in large lettering below the diagram a motto that could help you stop 'I-obsessions'.

Task 3: A solution to your lack of confidence is to change your binocular effects

When you look through binoculars you only see part of a horizon, But you think you can see it all. In relationships you get binocular effects when you:
* overstate how embarrassing and stupid your behaviour was;
* make assumptions about what was really going on;
* maximise the meaning of criticisms;
* read people's minds;
* see things in simple black and white terms; and
* see a small defect as a huge problem.

Question 5:   Look back at the example of the pop singer in Task 2. Which of his thoughts do you think are just assumptions?

Question 6:   In difficult situations do you get any 'awfulising' and make assumptions?

Action

Make a drawing of binoculars. Write any examples of your assumptions or your tendency to make assumptions on the diagram.

Let us return now to consider the story of the person who was stood up, which we looked at, at the beginning of this chapter. I am sure you will see that the concept of 'binocular effects' which we have just examined, applies to her negative thoughts. Read her list of awful beliefs once again. Her first belief is a rating statement caused by making an assumption about the person who stood her up. 'It is awful, because he is a super person'. 'But would a super person play a dirty trick like that? No! of course not. He is just an ordinary immature messed-up character- perhaps like the rest of us, but a little bit less wonderful than we are!' Her second belief is an assumption. 'He couldn't have liked me' It is possibly wrong. Perhaps a freak accident or a misunderstanding has prevented them from meeting at the agreed venue. Her third belief is an 'I-Obsession'; 'I've just made a fool of myself'. She has made a fool of herself by agreeing to a date. Okay perhaps she has done something foolish-but you cannot be a fool just because you have been foolish! If you call yourself a fool for doing something stupid you will be making the kind of over-generalisation, which frequently causes lack of confidence. You will be seeing things in very black and white ways. Her fourth thought adds to her shame and loss of confidence. She states; 'Everyone will be looking at me in the geography class.' This thought is an example of mind reading and maximising of meaning. The mind reading aspect is that she assumes that if friends are having a laugh during the geography class, they will laughing at her. Then she maximises the meaning of this by thinking that if they were laughing at her it would mean that their view of her was really terrible.

Task 4: To break out of circular thinking

I hope you are managing to see how the Rational Emotive/Cognitive analysis of thoughts really does help you to challenge upsetting conclusions. A final useful technique I can show you in this chapter is the 'vicious circle diagram'. A young man told me he was feeling unconfident. He had not successfully dated a member of the opposite sex for quite some time. He told me he felt unconfident. 'Ah' he said, 'the problem is that girls like confident men'. 'Let's see that as being a vicious circle' I said. 'See my diagram. Notice how your thinking just destroys your confidence. You do yourself down by getting yourself stuck in a circle of reasoning'

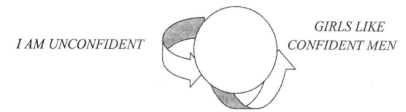

I AM UNCONFIDENT
GIRLS LIKE CONFIDENT MEN

'Your thinking just goes round and round and you torture yourself without really asking yourself if the evidence is good. When you say girls like confident men- is that perhaps a stereotype? If you felt just a little more confident that might be quite acceptable to many girls. Perhaps many girls get frightened away by men who seem arrogant or just socially superior to them. But in your situation your negative belief about girls causes you to become totally unconfident. Then you do nothing, you dry up in social situations, and don't manage to really get onto the starting blocks, far less get into the races'. The truth is that in life we often have to try to break out of circular thinking. Notice that circular thinking does not lead us to think objectively about evidence, or consider other ways of looking at things. Instead it leads us to be perfectionistic-which means that we feel we have to be at our best all the time. Anything less than a perfect performance will not be considered good enough by other people!

Question 7:   Can you think of any occasion when you got stuck in a pattern of circular thinking? One way of checking if you are using circular thinking is to write out all your thoughts about a problem either in a Cognitive diary or in a Rational Self Analysis form which we will examine below.

Task 5: Learn to Use a Rational Self Analysis

A Rational Self Analysis (RSA) is like an ABC form (See chapter 5).In a RSA you try to list all your thoughts-not just the key thoughts. The RSA helps you work on whirlpools and binocular effects by having another section called (D) for Debate in which you argue and dispute each of the beliefs at (B).

Study the example Rational Self Analysis form below and try to write in an argument against each of the points made at (B). At this point it is useful to explain why the heading BELIEFS is used in Rational Emotive therapy instead of THOUGHTS. A belief is a thought (or collection of thoughts) which is phrased so that its' full meaning becomes clearer and any implications are accurately stated. A belief is therefore a paraphrasing of thoughts. The beliefs, which, you write up in a RSA. form should correspond to the thoughts you felt you had, but they may be reworded to focus the meaning of the thought more clearly.

In earlier chapters I suggested that depression relates a lot to discouragement, and that the ways we develop discouraged tendencies from youth help to perpetuate our depressive thinking style. This chapter has shown how negative thoughts and global self-ratings contribute significantly to causing a lack of confidence. Perhaps you have noticed from the work in this chapter that Rational Emotive terms are more inclined to be jargon laden whereas the earlier Cognitive terms are more exact and precise. The advantages of the less exact Rational Emotive approach are that the terms can be more colourful and colloquial. For this reason it is useful to get a flavour of Rational Emotive ways of looking at things. In later chapters I will compare the use of terms from both therapies. In the next chapters we will consider how global self-ratings also make us less competitive in life and more prone to suffering from stress and worry.

Rational Self-Analysis	
A: Activating Event I wanted to ask a girl out but left myself down by lacking the courage.	
B: Beliefs 1. It would have been far too embarassing particularly if I got refused.	**D: Debate** 1. Nonsense. These events are just seven-day wonders. Friends and others soon forget they ever happened.
2. There must be a right way of doing this and I don't know what it is.	2. This is just an 'I-obsession'. There is no right way of handling the situation.
3. I am perhaps a little fat and spotty.	3. This just draws me into a self-rating. The more I see myself as an attractive person, the more other people will view me as attractive.
4. She gave me a look of pity or contempt last time she saw me.	4. _____ _____
5. Now I feel angry at myself, and my hopeless style of dealing with the opposite sex is once again too obvious.	5. _____ _____ _____
C: Consequences Embarrassed, unconfident, discouraged, angry; these are the main feelings and consequences this has evoked.	**E: Emotional Change** Self-accepting and more confident.

Chapter 9
Becoming a Better
Sportsperson or Performer

Task 1: To consider the importance of competitiveness in life

There are so many ways in which we have to be competitive in life. We are competitive when we do exams. When we try to influence colleagues or our children we are competing with other influences. Right now I am trying to prove to you that this therapy is useful. Perhaps you have a very good novel lying on your bedside table. I am aware of competing for your attention. So this study of sportsmen and performers is very relevant to all of us. We all have to perform in the big arenas of life.

Sportspeople have to be adaptable. It is no good giving up when you go through a bad patch and lose form. Getting frustrated with yourself doesn't help if it makes you too self-critical. Similarly, people who want to be sporty mustn't give up just because they do badly. They still need to have goals. Perhaps they also need to look around and experiment with team sports and athletic activities. They have to try to find their ideal sport, or their niche - the role that suits them best, where 'they can make a difference'.

Task 2: To consider how rational emotive imagery can help

The technique of rational emotive imagery (REI) is a useful exercise for many different kinds of problems. It involves:
*   imagining a difficult situation fully;
*   using force in your mind; and
*   seeing the situation in a less negative way.

I want to pay attention here to why the technique is useful for sportsmen and performers:

* you use this technique to prepare for trouble spots during a game or a performance.
* it helps you change inappropriate feelings such as anxiety to appropriate ones such as concern and regret.
* it stops you getting into whirlpools of awfulising and 'I-obsessions' (see Chapter 8).
* it builds up your mental strength if used regularly (just like a body workout builds up your muscles).

Example

A sportsman is telling a Counsellor that he no longer enjoys training and his ability and form have deteriorated. The Counsellor asks him to close his eyes and think imaginatively about how things have gone wrong. What comes to mind? The sportsman says:

'I think I have an image of the manager disapproving of me. He thinks that I am big headed. It feels sad and awful.'

Then he was helped to work on his *awfulising*. He put force in his mind and thought:

'Just relax. Getting down on myself only hurts my game. I can stand the manager being annoyed. The goalposts won't fall on my head. I won't spend my time being obsessed with the problem'.

He then had to move on to using 'positive rational emotive imagery' and think about positive aspects of training and the game. These positive thoughts were put onto a hypnotherapy tape along with reassuring statements and self affirmations. (For hypnotherapy training see chapters 14 and 18). Notice that when you use the R.E.I. technique you can use force in your mind and employ 'Emotive' thinking. Statements like 'the goalposts won't fall on my head' are helpful not just because of their logic but because of the Emotive impact they have. They help you to feel more positive.

Task 3: To consider how an understanding of rational emotive behaviourist therapy helps you perform better

According to Ellis (the main writer of this therapy) your musts and your awfulising just demoralise you. So change your 'musts' to preferences e.g. 'I prefer to do well.' I think this helps you to become non-competitively highly competitive! What this means is that you really want to do well but you don't have to! It is a good emotive statement that makes you a better team player.[4]

Suppose during a drama performance you make a slight mistake. Instead of worrying about your mistakes being noticed, you think about how you helped the whole team to do well and how the overall performance was very good.

You managed to think like this because of changing your 'musts' about your own performance. Instead of worrying about being = 100 you were happy to settle for being = 50. After the mistake, your morale did not collapse. Instead you retained your competitive attitude. With good self-esteem and the right kind of competitive attitude you stop rating yourself, getting frustrated and feeling that each opportunity in life is make or break.

Example

Our young shop assistant, Mandy, has had to work on this tendency to see things as make or break and therefore getting nervous and frustrated with herself. She has been able to write a de-awfulising exercise which helped her to overcome nervousness at interviews.

Question 2: Now use the de-awfulising column below and try to change each of the negative thoughts that Mandy has outlined above. Look back to the work done in previous chapters so that you are able to use both rational emotive and cognitive analysis to help you argue against each thought.

A: Activating Event	B: Awfulising	C: Consequence
I always get nervous at interviews I have an interview coming up so I will try to solve this problem.	1. This is make or break. 2. I will only have myself to blame if I do badly. 3. If I make a stupid response I will feel stupid and think that they were shocked by my stupidity. 4. The manager advised me to get some interview training. This means she thinks I am poor at interviews.	I feel nervous about the forthcoming interview.

D: De-awfulising
1. _____
2. _____
3. _____
4. _____

Task 4: To consider the behaviourist aspects of therapy

The other aspect of REBT is the behaviourist one. This is based on the scientific understanding that the body quickly gets conditioned to respond immediately to events. For example, if you saw a bull coming towards you as you walked through a field you would quickly feel scared and suddenly find that you either had tremendous energy to help you escape, or else you perhaps would become paralysed with fear. In many situations in life our nervous system triggers fear or anxiety reactions. We can however manage these unwanted reactions during sporting events by talking calmly to ourselves. This is called self-talk. To return to our example of the athlete who was helped by Michael Bernard (see Task 2), the self-talk statements below were developed by the athlete to help him control his anxiety during games:

* Concentrate on what I'm supposed to do next.
* No negative statements about myself.
* I believe in myself. I'm a good kick and mark.
* Relax, I'm in control. Take a slow, deep breath.

Action

If you find it hard to believe that self-talk helps, try it out in a game of 'Sister Sister'. This game involves a small group of people in much hilarity. The idea is to knock others out of the game by making them laugh. You just have to clasp hands as if in prayer and say, "Dear Sister [name], is it not indeed a sad and solemn occasion". Person replies, "Yes Sister [name] it is indeed a sad and solemn occasion". This person says it to another in the group. If students laugh they are out. You make the game funnier by using accents or suggesting silly things that have caused the situation to be a sad and solemn one. After you have done the game once try it with self-talk to see if that helps you do better. Use a sensible statement like "I don't have to laugh. I'm grown up and this is just silly".

Task 5: To make a record of your use of psychology to improve your performing in sport, drama, exams, or any of the other competitions of life

Write below about the trouble spots you can imagine yourself having when you perform. For example, just before, during and at the climax.

_____

_____

_____

Make a record of your use of REI. For instance, take one example (a), imagine it fully and note your awful thoughts. Then (b) use force in mind and (c) change the thoughts to calm ones.

Awfuls:_____

_____

_____

Now use positive imagery so that you imagine yourself coping very well with the event. Describe your imaginary thinking below.

_____

_____

_____

Now make up self-talk statements for use during difficult events to help you cope with anxiety, fear, nervousness and stress.

This chapter has shown how the use of emotive self-talk can really help you to do better in competitive situations. This is really important because many of us fail to overcome nervousness at interviews and therefore to make the kinds of important achievements that could turn our lives round and help us to overcome depression. Nervousness and anxiety also link with stress, and for this reason we will turn our attention to stress and depression in the next few chapters.

10

Stress - Links with Discouragement

Task 1: To investigate what causes our stresses

Most people think that stress is caused by overwork. This is only part of the story. In reality it is linked to a lot of different reactions and pressures. For example, some people

*   get stressed out because of always being excitable;
*   become too intense through nervousness or anxiety;
*   don't treat their bodies right and chase fun at any price;
*   insist on getting their work or house absolutely right;
*   are obsessed with living up to other people's expectations;
*   are tired and miserable because of problems at home;
*   leave things to the last minute then rush like mad;
*   don't take time to really understand things, they just drift;
*   have a nervous tendency to see important things as really big;
*   have no sense of their own values so they just join the rat race.

Tick the examples above if they apply to you right now or could do in the future.

Many people think that the way to deal with stress is to relax. There are different ways to relax, for example:

*   Progressive Relaxation
*   Taking exercise
*   Having a bath
*   Meditation
*   Massage
*   Guided fantasy

Task 2: One way to relax is through progressive relaxation

If you want to try it, here's how:

The teacher or student should read out the following instructions:

1.   Place your head and arms down on the desk or lean back on your chair. Close your eyes and just relax.

2.   Focus your attention on your toes. Tighten your toes and ankle. Tighter, tighter. Now relax them, relax, relax.

3.   Now your lower legs - tighten them. Okay, just relax the lower legs, the knees, and the upper legs, relax, relax.

4.   Imagine yourself looking down on a beautiful garden and the air is so lovely and fresh.

5.   Now tighten your tummy and chest. Tighter, tighter. Now relax, relax. Relax your internal organs and your lungs. Relax your spine and your ribs.

6.   When I say the word 'now' you will experience progressive relaxation. It will progress from your legs into your chest and your lower body will become fully relaxed. Ready now.

7.   Now tighten your arms. Tighter, tighter. Okay relax, relax, relax them. Feel the insides of your hands and the outsides of your hands relaxing. Now your arms.

8.   Tighten your head. Tighter, tighter. Now feel your cheeks and your neck, your nose and your mouth relaxing. Your forehead and scalp are relaxing. Above all, your eyes and the muscles around them need to relax.

9.   When I say 'now', your whole body will relax and your mind will close down. Now.

10.   Leave people relaxed in silence for 60 seconds.

11.   When I count to 5 you will come out of relaxation feeling tired but slowed down and de-stressed. 1, 2, 3, move your hands now; 4 and 5, open your eyes.

The attempt to manage stress by relaxing can be termed a behaviourist technique because you are trying to influence your conditioning. However we must turn now to the question of whether stress is caused by our tendencies to 'awfulise' and think in global ways about our failings.

Task 3: To Understand What the Rat Race is and to learn that it is only for Rats!

Lots of folk understand that there is a rat race out there where people work long hours and feel obliged to do more and more. In the rat race you only count if you rate. Are you clever? Are you very organised? Are you hard working? Other qualities don't always rate.

Not everybody joins the rat race. There are many sympathetic bosses who look after their workers etc., but out there somewhere the rate race goes on, and some people can't stop themselves joining it and fully approving of its values.

There are also many peer groups out there. In these peer groups you can be labelled a geek if you show a positive attitude to work. You can be seen as unsociable if you do not accept norms of drinking heavily, being witty all the time, etc. Notice once again that people in peer groups may have superficial attitudes in which you are a rateable commodity.

Not everyone approves of the peer group rat race. There are many sincere people who can become trusted friends, but the rate race is still out there. There are ways in which we all approve of it, but we will be much less stressed out if we don't fully approve of it.

Task 4: To find out how to escape the rat race

Many people manage to live their lives effectively without being sucked into the values of the rat race. There are several ways to do this:
*   Stop seeing a failure as awful.
*   Identify with better values, perhaps from religion or philosophy (see Chapter 19).
*   Use the rational emotive approach of looking at how we make awful statements which are too global and extreme.

The exercise below is called a 'de-awfulising exercise'. It is a little similar to the rational self analysis exercise which was described in Chapter 8, except that in this exercise you look for any 'awful' statements. You write the ABC form across the page because you want to deal with only a few key thoughts relating to the stresses and other negative feelings.

Example

A student considered what her awful thoughts and feelings were about exams that she would be sitting quite soon. She filled in an ABC form and then disputed and debated her negative thoughts.

A: Activating Event	B: Thoughts	C: Consequences
I will get more anxious as the exam gets closer. Then I will do badly.	1. I will have no excuse for my lack of effort 2. People will think badly of me. 3. Sometimes I find the work hard or boring 4. If I do badly it will be shameful.	The consequence of the situation is I feel anxious and unsure of myself.
D: Debate of Thoughts		
1.I suppose the worries and the sense of the bigness of the work do account for my problem so I do have some excuse. 2. Teachers and parents often realise that students have difficulties with the high standards of senior school work. 3. If I just relax and stop worrying about results, I can overhaul problem subjects more skilfully. 4. It is not shameful because lots of students have the same problems. A human being is worth far more than just his ability to learn things.		

Clearly the example above of an ABC form for the person who was worried about exams shows how the 'I-obsessions' and self ratings we studied in Chapter 8 were major problems. Look again at the Debate column. The first argument in this column is about changing the idea that there is no excuse for having this stress-related problem. This helps the person to escape from the I-obsession - the person has an excuse just because the negative feelings are indeed difficult to deal with. The second debating thought has to do with changing the assumption that teachers won't understand - this again can be seen as an assumption (a binocular effect). The third debating thought relates to reducing the tendency to emphasise the bigness of the situation. It may remind you of the concept of 'being non-competitively highly competitive' outlined in Chapter 9. The last debating thought is clearly about changing a Rating statement: 'I cannot be a stupid person for doing stupid things'.

At this point it may be very helpful for you to compare the REBT kinds of negative thought patterns with the CBT list which you read about in Chapter 2. Point number 1 on the ABC form can be termed an all or nothing error. Point number 2 can be described as being an expectation that other people such as teachers, will use black and white thinking and have negative attitudes to the student. I think you will find it helpful to continue trying to compare the negative thought patterns because in some respects the CBT ones are very useful. For example, black and white thinking is a very helpful description of the way people think in judgemental ways.

Imagine you were taking part in an interview for a really good job, but early on in the interview you answered a question very badly. This may have been because you were nervous initially. However, you now tell yourself; 'My chance is gone. I was so stupid. The interviewer must think I'm a fool.' Notice that an assumption you made about your interviewer has caused your morale to plummet. But your negative expectations were perhaps that the interviewer would see things in black and white ways. So the idea of black and white thinking helps you to get more insight into how you and other people can develop negative expectations and also negative attitudes. These negative attitudes can be overcome. For example, the interviewer could well think to himself, 'My interviewee certainly gave a very poor answer to my first question, but probably she is still very nervous. Let's not read too much into one mistake.'

While this chapter has focused more on REBT in dealing with stress and discouragement, I also wish to point out that the examples of cognitive therapy dealt with earlier are also relevant. By the time you have worked through this book I am sure that you will have clear ideas about how to use all the self-help exercises which are common to both of the cognitive therapies.

Chapter 11
Stress of Exams and Other Big Events

Task 1: To review progress and achievement

Write an account of how well or how badly you are coping with big events in your life.

_____

_____

_____

Task 2: To consider the basic problems you have faced in revising for exams or preparing for big events

To investigate the roots of any problems you should use the 'options on hold' (OOH) technique. As an example, let's consider a problem a boy had pumping up his bike tyre. He asked himself, 'Why isn't the pump working?' He considered all the options on the cause of the problem:

(a)   Do I have a slow puncture?
(b)   Is there a problem with the valve?
(c)   Is the problem in the tube?
(d)   Is the pump broken?

Another boy had problems preparing for exams. He did an OOH and considered each aspect of the problem in order:

(a)   Is the problem a long time before the exam, e.g. poor notes?
(b)   Is the problem in the weeks before the exam - revising?
(c)   Is the problem just before and during exams e.g. nervousness?
(d)   Is the problem worse half way through or after the event?

Now do an OOH for one of your own problems:

Problem

_____

_____

Long term
Aspect 1

_____

Aspect 2

_____

Short term
Aspect 3

_____

Aspect 4

_____

Aspect 5

_____

Aspect 6

_____

Task 3: To learn how to focus and operationalise key aspects of problems

Your next technique is OIP's which stands for operationalise important problems. To operationalise is to find an aspect of a problem that:
- (a) can be analysed easily;
- (b) can be operated on; and
- (c) would make a difference if it were changed.

So decide on an aspect on which you want to focus. You might like to work on it using a mind map. Look back to see the example of the mind map William was helped to construct in Chapter 3.

Now check out the 'ebb and flow' of this:

1. Are stress-type factors at play, e.g. frustration, pessimistic moods, nervousness, uptightness?
2. Are there knock-on effects from domestic or peer group problems?
3. Are there trigger factors e.g. you get angry with yourself and that increases frustration and self-doubt?

Task 4: To consider if beliefs are a drain on energy and therefore a cause of stress

People become unconfident because they have some of the following bad beliefs and they don't keep in mind the good beliefs.

Bad Beliefs
* Embarrassing things are so awful.
* If I do bad things I'm an awful person.
* If a person thinks badly of me, it's awful.

Good Beliefs
* There is nothing to be ashamed about in life.
* A person who does something bad or foolish is not a bad person.

Question 1:   Why are the bad beliefs bad for you?
                Why are the good beliefs good for you?

Okay, so you agree that there are good and bad beliefs. Now which of the following do you think are good beliefs and which of them are bad?
* I should be successful in life.
* I've got to do as well as possible.
* If everyone was disappointed in me I would probably feel a bit ashamed.

Would preference beliefs be better for you? These might include, 'I prefer to do well' or 'I would really like to do my best'.

Now play the rating card game in which you decide which cards are rational beliefs and which are not.

Rating Card Game	
To be happy in life you just have to make good choices.	Showing off is necessary because in life you have to be on top.
I am okay and I like myself just the way I am.	Everybody is equal. There are no superior people.
Rating card I rate = 0.	A bully is not a horrible person, just proud or defensive.
You have to find success of some kind in life.	It is too difficult to work and also enjoy yourself.
It is best to work hard all the time.	Parents should not interfere in our lives.

Doing something bad is silly but it doesn't make you a bad person.	Doing stupid things makes you a fool.
I must be popular and cool. It is awful to be slagged off.	Having a good drink is necessary for confidence.

Task 5: To consider why it is so important to relax the mind.

My key idea here is that we all get stress 'wind ups' - but some get it worse than others. What happens is that negative feelings make negative thoughts pop up. These thoughts then justify and reinforce the negative feelings. This is called 'emotional reasoning'. It is a key concept for the cognitive therapies. Think for a minute about why this idea is so significant. The theory suggests that if we get certain feelings, these feelings make negative thoughts come into our minds. These negative thoughts can be called 'automatic thoughts' because our feelings draw us into having them. The mind then can be seen as being very prone to propaganda and bias. Negative feelings create a propaganda network. The automatic thoughts that are the result of emotional reasoning are termed 'self-talk'.

Consider the kinds of Self-Talk people who are stressed employ:

* 'I've got to hurry up.'
* 'I can only give myself half an hour maximum to do this because I have other work to do.'
* 'This is so tiring, difficult and frightening'
* 'I am totally hopeless at coping.'

By contrast, think how a relaxed person approaches revision and other big events:
* 'Take your time - there is no rush'
* 'Let's try to understand this carefully.'
* 'I'll just do my best.'

Task 6: You can relax by changing your stress induced self-talk

Look back at your OOH. work in Task 2. Can you see how stress-induced self-talk acts as a trigger for frustration and anxiety? Consider the sorts of calming self-talk that could help you in some of the following problem situations. Then try thinking out good self-talk for your problem situations.

(a) You are about to go into a difficult exam. Your friends seem confident.

(b) You are about to ask out a member of the opposite sex.

(c) You are refereeing a football match and the players are making some crunching tackles.

Task 7: To consider how far your daily routines help you relax

(a) Which of your daily activities cause stress, e.g. they tire you out, get you too excitable or too worked up?

_____

(b) Which of your daily routines has the most positive effects, causing relaxation?

_____

(c) Which of your daily routines has negative effects, causing stress?

_____

(d) What changes would really make a difference?

_____

(e) What new routines would you like to add to your lifestyle? For instance, get up earlier so you can relax over breakfast, do progressive relaxation, take up yoga.

_____

Task 8: Now your action plan

After doing an OOH and OIPs you do an AP! (action plan).

Make a list of things you can do differently and the key things you have learned about dealing with stress and your ways of studying or coping with big events.

_____

_____

_____

_____

_____

_____

_____

_____

_____

Chapter 12
Anger and Depression

It would be nice if we could cope with the harsh blows of life wouldn't it? Many people don't. We get stuck in feelings of anger a lot of the time. Then it spills out in family rows, marital conflict, road rage and society gets more and more obsessed with law and order, discipline, back to basics, etc - real hang'em and flog'em stuff. But how come we tend to get the anger tendency? One reason people suffer from anger is that they have not fully realised just how much trouble the anger tendency can get them into. It can cause some very damaging and self-defeating behaviours. Another reason is that people are quite unaware that the anger tendency has links with the way our attitudes have developed. People acquire attitudes from various quarters in life. Perhaps, as a teenager, anger was very useful, to help us get some control over other difficult teenagers. Then we learned to feel good about having a powerful nature. It helped us to become confident and able to fit in well. However, in a later stage of life the anger tendency may not be so useful. It may cause us to behave in ways that cause bad relationships or bad experiences. As a result of that we may become depressed.

One problem is that from childhood we have been moulded by the ideals we pick up. We may learn from parents and peers the importance of being perfect, which is about looking good and having high achievements. Or we may get indoctrinated with the overriding ideal of being good. Sometimes we deal with the humiliations of life by developing a big 'be strong mentality'. This can make us seem macho or dominant over others. Not only are we conditioned to conform to one or two of these ideals but in the process we are conditioned to make other people conform as well. The 'be good' ideal makes us critical of the world: 'It's a bad place and lots of people are not nice'. The 'be perfect' ideal can make us critical of other people's performances and any sign of imperfections in others. The 'be strong' ideal can lead us to be angrily dismissive of others or critical of them if they come across as false or insincere.

None of this makes us lean and efficient in the way we operate our ideals. Instead it makes us unsympathetic and demanding. We don't, for example, take account of how other people have evolved into having different ideals from us.

Example

Let us reconsider the problems faced by my client William. Look back over the concreteness search work which was done to help William in Chapter 3. What do you think seem to be his main problems? Clearly anger and critical attitudes do play a part in his relationship. Perhaps it is worthwhile for us to explore the theme of anger with him again.

Counsellor: Welcome back William, how are you? And how have things been since we last met? (door opener)

William: Things are still very difficult. John is still waking up at night. The work we did together was helpful though, and has made me feel more aware of the way my family problems have developed.

Counsellor: So things have been difficult this week. (reflection of content)

William: Yes, on Tuesday night there was a royal row. John woke us both up in the early morning. Mary told him that if he wasn't a good boy mummy would leave home. John just went into a temper tantrum. Mum started to pack her case. I could see she was terribly stressed. I had to try to calm things down. I stuck a video on for John. Then I spent an hour trying to talk Mary down. I advised her to come with me to counselling.

Counsellor: So Tuesday was a tough night for you. You look anxious and upset, how do you feel about it now? (open-ended question)

William: I'm feeling quite worn out. It doesn't matter how hard I try, things don't go forward. John still acts like a spoilt child. Mary says she won't go to counselling. I feel I'm trying to move mountains and am just getting myself stressed out.

Counsellor: You feel anxious, and you try hard to get things sorted out but you just end up feeling stressed out. (reflection of feeling)

William: Yes, things are just not fair.

Counsellor: 'Not fair - what does that mean to you? (chaining question)

William: I'm just really angry at Mary, I suppose. She packs her bag and talks about leaving one minute and the next she says she doesn't need counselling.

Counsellor: How does that make you feel? (chaining question)

William: It feels like she is saying, 'I don't value this marriage. It is not worth my time or effort to work at it.'

Counsellor: That must be a horrible feeling for you - like it is very sad and undermining for your morale. (additive empathy)

William: Yes, I don't know where I stand any longer.

Counsellor: Let's put these thoughts and feelings onto an ABC form, William, so we can see them more clearly. (concreteness search)

Counsellor: Can you think of any more thoughts that you could add to the Beliefs column, William? (concreteness search)

GLOSSARY: Additive Empathy

Additive empathy is when a counsellor tries to see the implications of what the client has been telling him. He shows he can see how a client would tend to feel because of the effect of a problem on him. This attending to the client's feelings is very important the reasons for it have been explained in Chapter 1. It is necessary to really understand a client's feelings before you try to challenge his/her perspective. The example above shows how the client's anger is quite excusable. You or I could feel the same way in such difficult circumstances. So additive empathy is when a counsellor:

*   shows a logical implication of how a client feels;
*   considers the general picture and draws the client's attention to overlooked aspects; and
*   compares different themes to help a client make new insights.

A: Activating Event	B: Beliefs	C: Consequences
Wife refuses to come to counselling.	1. It means she doesn't want to work on the marriage.	Feels angry, rejected, sad, depressed and anxious.

William: Yes, I think I am saying that she doesn't have any excuse for not wanting to work on the problems.

Counsellor: Okay William, could we look at a pro and con exercise for that idea that she has no excuse. (challenge)

Pro (no excuse)	Con (there is an excuse)
1. Our marriage is in a mess, as she has talked about leaving.	1. The problems we have are more about John than about us.
2. She refuses to come to counselling, so she doesn't care.	2. The death of our first child was a huge problem. Perhaps we never got over it.
3. She doesn't talk honestly about her feelings.	3. We are both so uptight about dealing with children.
4. She over-reacts with John.	
5. If I say that to her she says I just nag.	4. After the cot death we just didn't really talk about grief. I was so busy at work I left it to her mum to talk. It is not a man's role.
6. She thinks I spoil John.	

The pro and con exercise helped William to reconsider whether perhaps his views about Mary were once again a little extreme. The exercise helped him to reduce his feelings of being rejected. Instead he realised that he should try to support Mary. He worked out that perhaps she just feels like a failure as a mother and simply doesn't want to expose herself to criticism by going to counselling. The pro and con exercise can help people to reduce anger. It can also help people to work on discouragement, as we saw in Chapter 2 when we considered Mandy's problems with having an appraisal.

Anger therefore involves making an assumption that the people who are doing wrong 'have no excuse' for their behaviour.

Another guideline that is sometimes true about anger is to see it as a 'scream of outrage' that draws us into extreme thinking. A lady described her mum as a heavy drinker. One of her thoughts was: 'She is always pretending there is nothing wrong and puts on a stupid act of being a really good person - in fact a very special lady.'

Once again the counsellor could challenge the negative thought by asking a standard question: 'You feel there is no excuse for this very irritating behaviour but could we consider for a while if there may be any possible way of excusing her?'

When we go on assertiveness training courses we are taught to be assertive (not angry). It is important to know why this general rule is sensible. Firstly, anger is less constructive because it draws people into angry feuds. If you try to get someone over the barrel of a gun, he/she just tends to resent your power. Secondly, anger can drive another person deeper into the whirlpool of guilt and shame-perpetuating depressive 'acting out' - they become more inclined to have another drink, put it on the horses, etc. Your anger makes you sound unsympathetic just at a time when the other person's morale is at rock bottom. You did more than simply criticise - you rubbed things in.

Sometimes our anger is particularly unconstructive because it incorporates a scream of unhappiness that states: "Look what you have done to me. I can't possibly be happy now.' This can be described as being a binocular effect. With binoculars you only see part of the horizon. The view you have of the horizon makes the whole situation look impossibly awful.

Examples

I helped a businessman who was in the middle of a vital deal when he and his partner fell out. I used an ABC form so that in column A I outlined the activating event (which was the disagreement over the deal). Then I wrote down his feelings in column C and then his thoughts in column B. That ABC form is shown below, because it gives an illustration of the scream of unhappiness, and the binocular effects I referred to above.

ABC Form		
A: Activating Event	B: Thoughts	C: Feelings
This deal has been badly handled	1. He is listening to all the wrong people and ignoring me.	Upset, angry, depressed, worried.
	2. He should be more sensible at his age.	
	3. I am practically at the point of breakdown. The right deal means so much to me. My whole future is at steak.	
	4. His stupid decisions are wrecking my life!	

I then helped him to change his thoughts by using column D for Debate. Drawing on the insights above into how anger involves combining a 'scream of unhappiness' with assumptions and other binocular effects, I considered each of his thoughts. To deal specifically with point 3, I asked him to consider how he could still find happiness if things in fact went badly. Then I asked him if he could get his business friend to talk to a colleague who could give better advice so that the best possible judgements were in fact made regarding the situation.

The ABC form helped to reduce the panic and then he got his head working again and became his usual robust, assertive self. The problem was soon resolved because he had escaped from the angry 'doom and gloom' mentality.

Anger can draw people into over-generalisations and assumptions. An RSA form can help us to work on the network of anger and other negative feelings and thoughts. Below is an RSA form which was developed by my other client, Mandy. See if you can complete the sections of the D (Debate) column which she has not filled in yet.

A: Activating Event - I caught herpes three years ago. It is incurable, but I get treated with medicine that has side effects. Having herpes gets me down sometimes.	
B: Beliefs	**D: Debate**
It is disgusting. I'd hate to let a boyfriend know I had it.	People have worse things.
2. I am sometimes wary of getting drawn into relationships and herpes plays a part in that.	2. Getting a sexually transmitted disease can happen to anybody.
3. I was quite silly as a teenager. Having herpes seems to remind me how I was a pain. I ended up getting an abortion which was disgraceful.	3. _____ _____ _____ _____ _____
4. I was into silly lads when I was at school. Now I don't trust men so easily. I can get paranoid and huffy with men.	4. _____ _____ _____ _____
C: Consequences	**E: New Feelings**
I feel unconfident. It is sad that I get down about things.	

As we have seen in this chapter, anger is often a cause of depression because it prevents us from acting effectively in relationships. Sometimes anger is linked directly with depression. It can involve a 'scream of outrage' which states, 'Because of you I can never be happy'. Clearly, anger can be justified and it can at times be constructive, but we have to be aware of its destructiveness and the importance of being very careful about our angry moods and their potential effects on other people.

Chapter 13
Learn to be Assertive

Task 1: To consider the meaning of assertiveness

There are three ways of behaving in terms of relating to others: being aggressive, being submissive, being assertive.

Assertiveness is in between the submissive and aggressive styles. Assertive people try to be firm but not unreasonable. They try to be calm and give good reasons when they make requests. They work to improve confidence and manage anger. They try to have a sense of their own rights but also their responsibilities and the kinds of rules that make life okay for everybody. When people fail to act assertively there may be several reasons for it. Firstly, they may lack the kinds of knowledge that help them to adopt an assertive lifestyle. Secondly, they may be blocked in some way from acting assertively. Lastly, their morale may be too low for them to have the courage and composure to sound assertive.

Task 3: The importance of anger management

Anger gets in the way of assertiveness in the following respects. It stops you being accurate when you are criticising others. It moves you more towards bias and unfairness. Wouldn't it be better to foster a good relationship by having an atmosphere in which you show that you value people even when you have to disagree or criticise? Certainly if you are specific, forceful and reasonable in making requests and criticisms you are less likely to face constant opposition. Another aspect to this is that anger is often a result of embarrassment or humiliation. At such times, anger does not help a person because the real problem is a lack of confidence and low self-esteem.

Task 4: To consider some specific techniques

Below is a list of techniques for being assertive which you can try out later:

*   Giving a compliment before making a criticism.
*   Broken record - Like a record, which repeats itself, you keep repeating your request.
*   Fogging - Like fog you become inscrutable sometimes. You don't have to reveal your views if you are just likely to be attacked.
*   Checking things out - This is when you inquire into what is on another person's mind, i.e. how fair do things seem?
*   Workable compromise - This involves coming up with a solution that might suit all the people involved.
*   Recycled assertion - Either you or someone else is getting annoyed, so you return to the calm, assertive style later.
*   Escalation assertion - You gradually up the ante.
*   Being congruent - This is when your non-verbal style is suited to the communication that you are making. You don't look two-faced or weak. You are also able to receive other people's views fairly and considerately.
*   Being positive - People take to folk who like them, compliment them, and try not to be huffy or hypercritical.

Task 5: Body language and assertiveness

Try to think of one situation in which it is difficult to be assertive. Then consider the technique of being congruent below.

Body language reveals the inner mood, and inappropriate body language reinforces inappropriate mood. For example, if your eyes often look down at the floor this reinforces low faith in oneself, or timidness or shyness. Below are some examples of non-verbal language showing how to get it right.

*   Posture: Upright but leaning slightly towards the other person.
*   Distance: Not too close or too far away.
*   Eye contact: Relaxed, but not gazing or persistent.
*   Mouth: Jaw relaxed, friendly smile but only smile if appropriate.
*   Voice: Warm and relaxed even if the tone is raised.

*   Gestures: Body fairly still, as fiddling can convey nerves or boredom.

*   Speech: Not mumbling but speaking very clearly.

*   Relative position: Relaxed, not ready to rush away but appearing ready to be persistent, sensitive, good humoured, negotiating or decisive as the situation requires.

Task 6: Being assertive with young children

Parents often find that their relationships with young children can descend into a battle of wills. It seems that the only solution sometimes is to accept the difficulties until the child gets to be just a little older and wiser. However, with some children the battle of wills doesn't have to end in defeat for the parents. Some young children respond well to techniques such as 'time-out'. This is when a naughty child is removed to the front door or some other corner and told to stay there until his/her punishment is over. If the child yells and screams then his/her time-out only starts from when he/she calms down. Another technique is to set a time limit, for example, 'we will play at the park for five more minutes only'. A very useful technique is distraction. Humour is a great tool for distracting youngsters. I have a joke I use with a certain young relative. When he objects to being taken to bed, I use my joke to distract him. I say to him, 'You are not putting me in a case'.

Task 7: Considering how we get blocked from being assertive

When parents have a variety of depressing concerns, their energy and confidence can both be low, and this then prevents them from enjoying the challenge of taking part in the daily ritual of having some control over their children. Sometimes their morale is so low that they fail to realise that they do succeed at least some of the time. Even the achievement of building a friendly and loving relationship with a young child is an Assertiveness success story.

Sometimes, though when people feel that they have been blocked from acting assertively, they can easily check out the reasons for this using an ABC form. People are often blocked from acting assertively because they worry too much about other people's reactions or about how they will feel. For example, Mary is concerned about her father. He smokes too much and she has noticed that he get bouts of bronchitis from time to time. He always seems to be coughing. She feels she should encourage him to give up smoking but she finds it difficult to discuss. Below is an ABC form of what she thinks and feels.

A: Activating Event	B: Beliefs	C: Consequences
Dad smoking	1. I feel it would kind of make him feel silly if his teenage daughter gave him lessons on how to stop smoking. 2. He wouldn't listen anyway. 3. I'll just get annoyed with him, and that would not be fair. 4. It's none of my business.	I feel sorry for him.

Now work on D below - better ways of seeing things, for example, try to change each thought.

D: Debate
1. _____
2. _____
3. _____
4. _____

William has difficulties saying 'no' to his friends. They want him to stay out late at night and they tell him to lie to his parents about it. Complete the ABC form below to tackle this problem:

A: Activating Event	B: Beliefs	C: Consequences
Friends put me under pressure to misbehave.	1. I'd look a right fool if I said no. 2. A few late nights do no harm. 3. I can't discuss this with my mum because I feel bad about it. 4. If I said no, my friends would just keep on persuading me anyway.	anxiety.

Now complete the D (for Debate) column below for William's problems.

D: Debate
1. _____ _____
2. _____ _____
3. _____ _____
4. _____ _____

Task 8: Working on self-acceptance

If you work at having good morale then you will find that you are more able to accept that in life you win some battles and lose others. Also, if you can see yourself as being = 50, then you won't invest too much pride in your assertiveness achievements. When morale is low, we sometimes try too hard and end up being aggressive. When we accept ourselves as flawed individuals who don't always come out on top in the struggles of life, then we make more allowances for other people not always behaving perfectly. Being anxious and nervous doesn't always help because these negative states make us demand immediate success, and if we don't get it we become discouraged. While fear is a cause of people being blocked from acting assertively (and we will deal with this

78

in the next chapter), low morale is also a cause. Therefore people need to accept themselves and accept the situation they find themselves in. (We will deal later with difficult situations in Chapter 18).

A technique for improving acceptance is the 'why things are okay' list. You could try using it in your cognitive diary booklet for your own situation. First, consider the examples below and see if thinking out a long list of positives helps with acceptance:

1. Imagine that as a result of a car accident you became blind. Make a list of the ways you could still be happy.
2. Imagine that you have become a single parent. List the reasons you can still be happy.
3. Imagine you have a difficult four year old. No matter what you do, you fail to win some of the battles of will. Make a list of the ways you can still feel good about yourself.
4. Imagine you have a difficult week coming up. Your schedule will become hectic and you will deal with some difficult people. You can calm yourself down by making a list of 'why things are okay today'.

Question 1: Could your morale be better? Could you use any of the assertiveness techniques to help you with a specific problem. Perhaps you could consider a situation in which you are blocked from being assertive and check out what is going wrong by using an ABC form.

Question 2: Consider our client William. Do you think that he would have found any part of this chapter useful for helping him deal with his problems? When clients benefit from reading useful material the counselling approach is called bibliotherapy. So it is very useful for people who are undergoing cognitive counselling to read articles and books that teach about the therapy.

Many people think of assertiveness as training in using power effectively. In actual fact it is training in sharing power and overcoming the blocks that prevent us from having a share of that power. This chapter makes the surprising but nevertheless correct claim that being a success in terms of assertion on just one-third of occasions is quite sufficient, and that taking a relaxed approach to being assertive helps us to overcome aggression, anxiety and low morale. Most psychologists think we are more aggressive than we often realise. If we work at being more reflective about our aggressive tendencies and are willing to take ownership of the problem, then we can become better at using the skill of being assertive. When we work at sharing power instead of trying to grab as much of it as possible, then we find that other people are more willing to allow us to be assertive. They become less inclined to try to insult us or humiliate us and as a result our self-image and self-esteem can improve. Oddly enough, by trying less hard to be assertive we indeed can become much better at it.

Chapter 14
Fear and Depression

Task 1 To appreciate the links between fear and depression

William (our role-play client) has done some good work on his anger and his lack of assertiveness skills. However when he came to see me today he looked really quite stunned and shocked. Below you can read about his counselling interview.

Counsellor:William, you look down today. What's happened since I saw you last? (door opener)

William: I'm just feeling stunned. My stomach is in a knot. It's like I'm winded.

Counsellor: Something bad has really upset you. (reflection of feeling)

William: Yes, I'm just shocked and very anxious.

Counsellor: What's happened? (open-ended question)

William: Last night my wife told me that she intends to leave me in the next six months.

Counsellor: That's the worst news you could hear right now. (reflection of content)

William: Yes I just feel numb.

Counsellor: Numb? (minimal encourager)

William: Yes, it feels like I'm going to lose my beautiful wife, and my son will grow up thinking of me as a stranger a man who could not hold the marriage together, and who wasn't a good daddy. I will be lonely from now on, with only my humiliating family to relate to. It's all a kind of punishment, a life sentence.

Counsellor: That seems a pretty awful scenario, William. I can see that's what it seems like right now. But would it have to be like that? Is there anything about that scenario that you can doubt? (challenge)

William: Well, I met my wife when I was just 20. One minute I did not know any attractive women at all and the next I had bumped into her. Perhaps that shows me that you can't be sure what is round the next corner. But does that mean I won't have an awful life? I'm not sure.

Revision: Counselling Skills
Notice how the counselling approach of just showing empathy and allowing the client to experience his feelings and speak from his feelings has helped William to sense the nature of his anxieties about the future. His assumptions about the future were then gently challenged. He was given time to work through his depressed reasoning. Not long after the initial challenge, William was able to consider the question, 'Will my son see me as a'stranger' - a failure as a father?' This challenge worked surprisingly well and led to a change in William's depressed mood. It also alleviated his anxiety.

Task 2: To consider why cognitive theory also applies to fear

It has been found that negative thoughts really do stimulate the worry and bodily arousal that we associate with fear. This is because thoughts contribute to the emotional reasoning cycle we looked at earlier. In particular, our over-generalising thoughts cause lots of problems. This is because these thoughts involve us in exaggerating the importance of the problems we face. For example, we tend to use words like awful and terrible without realising that our emotions are then triggered by the possibility that we are about to face some kind of catastrophe. So for this reason we have to find and do some work on our 'awfulising thoughts'. With regard to fears, these thoughts usually involve predicting that something awful will happen. Also, people often get 'what if' thoughts which quickly bring semi-conscious scary images to mind; for example, 'What if I fell down this steep hill?' or 'What if I drowned?' So you just have to use the RSA technique (outlined clearly in Chapter 8) so that

A: Activating Event	B: Beliefs	D: Debate
My efficiency at work is reduced.	1. They have it in for me. What if I make a mistake this week?	1. These 'what ifs' don't help. I need more confidence, not worry. So cut it out.
	2. My image of them is scary. They can make a terrible fuss about small things.	2. A fuss only lasts 10 minutes so let's not overstate this problem. Just work at being efficient.
	3. The whole thing about going to work feels daunting.	3. The doors don't hit you as you go in. No, the job is fine.
	4. The company owes huge debts so we are all on edge.	4. The debt is £2 million but trade is now improving. We've had debts before. As long as I have an action plan for unseen difficulties such as redundancy and practice doing CVs then I can cope. I have skills to take to a new job.

you list your negative thoughts in column B and then try to debate them and dispute them in column D. See the example on the previous page of an RSA for a person who tended to worry a lot about work-related problems, and in particular the possibility of being made redundant.

Task 3: To consider the behaviourist aspect of treating fears

Nearly a hundred years ago, it was discovered that the best way to treat phobias was to use progressive relaxation (see Chapter 10) along with very relaxing music so that the nervous system's arousal could be calmed down. Using this technique, a client can be helped to write a list of the ways that his fears would affect him, from the worst examples to the least frightening. This is called a fear hierarchy list. Then the least frightening fear is introduced into the relaxed setting. For example, if a person is frightened of horses, perhaps a picture of a horse would be shown to them. Then he/she would be encouraged to use the progressive relaxation technique to reduce the arousal caused by the picture. This process of desensitisation would be continued until all the fears in the hierarchy had been dealt with.

Some people can use progressive relaxation very effectively to calm down the body arousal that contributes so much to anxiety states. However, there are other relaxing techniques that people may find they can do quickly, even when they are very busy and have insufficient time for progressive relaxation. Below are a variety of ways of relaxing and thereby calming down fearful thoughts.

Meditation technique

This is when you train your brain to slow down and cut out excited or anxious thoughts. You just have to relax at your desk and press against the area around the back of your neck and the top of your shoulders. Rub gently as if you were massaging it. Then breathe in deeply and say one word as you breathe out, perhaps the word 'peace' would do. Then breathe out and say another word to yourself, such as 'love'. Keep this going for a minute or two and then try to fade the words out so you say them more and more softly to yourself. Then try to have your mind completely empty, so you have no thoughts in it and the excited buzz of your brain can be reduced. Notice how this creates a very relaxed feeling. Try to remain in this relaxed state for a while.

Hypnotherapy

This is a method of influencing the unconscious mind by using auto-suggestions and visualisations. Tell yourself, "I am going way down deep, deep, deep into a trance. When I say 'now', my feet can relax. 'Now!' And the nicely coloured relaxation can flow through my body. 'Now!' I am just sitting on a flower, gently moving in the breeze. It's like being a rag doll, you just go limp, deep, d-e-e-e-p. I can see a tree with star fruit on it and when I taste the sweet taste of star fruit I will go deeper into trance. That's it - tasting the start fruit and going into trance". You can continue like this with your visualisation, for instance by drifting through a pleasant garden (See another example of this in chapter on Transitions).

Ways of slowing your body down

There are various ways of slowing your body down so that you get into a relaxed, less anxious state. Just having a bath is one example of this. Another one is to use light music. Try using the sink and swim exercise described in the Chapter 16. Another favourite of mine is the 'upside down experience'. To do this you just put your feet over the back of a chair or sofa and simply lie upside down like that for a while.

Task 4: To Consider how to combine various techniques effectively

One reason why people should learn to use the full variety of techniques from both the behaviourist and cognitive approaches is because, surprisingly enough, a technique that works well one minute may not be so effective the next. Let's take an example of a small child (perhaps your little brother) who suddenly finds his coping skills for fear don't seem to work.

Little Mike is being a real pain. He keeps getting up at night and wakes you up every time. He's a big boy now, so he shouldn't be frightened of the dark any more. You think to yourself, 'What's going on here? Is he too embarrassed to tell us what's bothering him? I'll sit down with him this evening and just show sympathy, give him a bit of affection, and ask him what's up.

That evening you find out that Mike has been very frightened recently by watching a scary television programme. He was so frightened by it that he couldn't even bear going to school by himself. You think to yourself, 'I will use the behaviourist techniques I read about in Chapter 9 and I will make him a poster which he can look at when he is getting ready to fall asleep.' Below is the poster that you used to help your little brother to get over his fear.

Fear Reduction Poster

DO THE FOLLOWING STEP BY STEP, WHILE TRYING TO GET TO SLEEP.

1. Breathe in, say 'stupid'; breathe out say 'peace'. Repeat five times.
2. Sink into bed and stop yourself thinking anything at all for 30 seconds.
3. Think of a nice place you would like to be in. *Use my little drawing opposite* to help you, or, when you have time, make up your own.
4. Think about why mum and dad are not frightened.
5. Tighten your head and chest as you count to 16. Now relax them as you count to 100. See if you feel sleepy.
5. If you don't feel sleepy, say to yourself, 'It's okay I can cope. I like myself just the way I am.' Then go back to the beginning and go through the list again. And keep doing it. No, don't get up to bother me. I'm trying to sleep

---

Task 5: To consolidate the lessons learned in this chapter

In my experience, people can use logic to gain some control over fear. I remember an incident when I had taken a class of students away for a few days to a youth hostel in the Highlands. Suddenly one night I found they were all very frightened. Youngsters were sitting around crying because they believed that a dangerous prowler was regularly coming to the hostel during the night. I asked them to think calmly and carefully about the situation. I told them that their minds were actually quite good at calculating risks: Each time you cross a road there is some risk. I asked them if there might be any other explanation for the reported incident that a man was seen late at night outside the hostel? I asked them if they thought being in the Highlands was more dangerous or less dangerous than being in the city. I then asked them if we could work out how to feel more in control and able to manage the risk so that they all felt safer. By thinking logically they were able to counteract their fearful assumptions.

I also recall helping a young man who was paralysed by fear (his hands were in fact stiff and tight) simply by doing a sink and swim exercise with him (see chapter 16). The exercise helped him to get in touch with his strong feelings and concerns and then to think them through effectively. The relaxing effect of the sink and swim exercise influenced his nervous system's arousal and helped to calm it down.

So in this chapter we have considered how working on the assumptions, the negative imagery and the body arousal all help to reduce fear. One important thing here is to help fearful people to improve their morale. When people suffer from extreme fear they feel quite out of control. It is hard for them to believe that any techniques can really help. However, knowledge does help. It counteracts this low morale problem. For example, it has been found that panic attack sufferers benefit from learning more about the nature of panic attacks. [5]According to McKay et al's self-help book Thoughts and Feelings, 'This is the most important fact to remember about panic - it can't last for more than three minutes if you stop scaring yourself with anxious thoughts.'

The lesson of this chapter is that fear, depression and low morale can all operate at an emotional level to draw a person into very negative conclusions about life and the problems they face. I hope the examples of cognitive therapy challenges in this chapter do help you to work on morale so that pessimism can be replaced by faith and self-belief. However, as this book is about depression, I have naturally kept this chapter on fear and depression reasonably brief. I would recommend reading McKay et al's cognitive therapy text mentioned above if you want to study the treatment of fear in more depth.

Question 1: Consider a situation which causes you some fear or anxiety. Then make up a set of memo cards containing good self-talk suggestions so that you can help yourself to cope with the experience. (see Chapter 9 for help with the development of self-talk suggestions.) or design a poster that helps you to cope with the fear.

Question 2: In what ways could the behaviourist techniques reported in this chapter be of help to our client William?

It might be useful for you to know that William has successfully resolved the anxiety and depression caused by his wife's suggestion that she would leave. As a result he is feeling quite positive about learning all he can about self-help therapies. William is of course, a role-play client, but the counselling examples are drawn from real-life counselling and self-counselling situations.

Chapter 15
Coping with Difficult Relatives

Task 1: To consider Bethune's advice in off the hook - Coping with addiction

How would you cope if one of your family was a drug addict? Bethune's book, *Off the Hook, Coping with Addiction*, points out that family members get so sad about the problem that it becomes like a family sickness. Their sadness makes them angry with the addict and then later they feel guilt about being angry. They suffer from emotional turmoil, with shame, grief, and envy (towards people who have few problems). Bethune's outlines her advice on coping with the shame, which causes such families to feel isolated from friends and relatives, in the extract below:

Shame just doesn't apply. If your child is suffering from an addiction, your child is ill. Addiction is no less an illness than diabetes or cancer. Would you feel shame if your child suffered from these. Mary and James are well-known citizens in their local community. Their daughter Sara figured largely in the local paper in a shoplifting charge (getting money for her addiction). But Mary and James knew their daughter was ill - not evil - and continued to hold their heads high, even managing to live sanely in the chaos created by her troubled daughter. As Mary put it:

1. *She has accepted that she has no control over anyone else's life but her own.*
2. *She has accepted that addiction is an illness not a moral sin.*
3. *She has given her daughter directions about where to get help and is keen to help her.*
4. *She has released her daughter - with love - to make her own decisions.*

*5. She has learned to live her own life not her daughter's.[8]
Bethune off the hook, coping with addiction.*

Question 1: If you had a child who was addicted, how would you cope? Complete the list of coping strategies below.

How best to deal with family problems

* Watch for the kinds of thoughts that cause you sadness and anger. Simply censor them. Put force in your mind to make them go away, and put a smile on your face. The more you act as if things are okay, the more things will be.

* Remember that you do actually have a right to enjoy your life! Instead of feeling guilty about trying to be happy, see yourself as a role model for the rest of the family to copy. When you focus on your right to have some happiness you become less angry with the ill drug addict and less easily depressed.

* Kick a ball against a wall vigorously or dig the garden to take your mind off things or help you get over the anger.

* Try to be good at spotting the feelings that people have and leave them alone if need be.

* Don't seek angry discussions, rub things in or nag all the time.

* Make allowances for people having different kinds of personalities, e.g. some are extroverted, some introverted, etc.

* Have a 'get up and go' attitude. You can get on with your life. You are not helpless just because of a family problem.

* _____

_____

* _____

_____

Task 2: To consider how important good relationships are for helping to deal with difficult youngsters

Research on why teenagers take up smoking, alcohol and drugs, in Britain, has acknowledged parental influence. But it has tended to concentrate on parent example. It has been believed that children learn from parents because a parent is a role model- indeed is the first and therefore most important role model for a growing child.

Yet recent studies have suggested that children's relationships with their parents might have a more direct effect on tobacco, alcohol and drug misuse, than any other factors. The parents' role of being a good sincere friend therefore may be every bit as important as their discipline role. This has big implications for how we best cope with youngsters when they are going through the difficult teenage years. Things which make us condemning, such as; anxieties, the need for social respectability, anger, extreme religious views, and perfectionistic parenting attitudes, will not help us to keep working on having a good relationship with our troubled child. This means that our religious or philosophic views need to be moderate and not too demanding. For this reason we need to consider religion and philosophy later in the final chapter of this book. The basic conclusion from modern research is that laying down the law isn't always the answer, but that keeping communication channels open is.

Question 1:   Do you think this research backs up Bethune's approach?

Task 3: To consider if families that develop counselling skills can best support their difficult child

Marlatt's[7] research on how 'drug addict' patients suffer relapses show us a picture of the typical drug addict, which is surprisingly human. The drug addict gets the same kind of emotional reactions and upsets as the rest of us. This is indeed surprising. The reason why many of us find it surprising is because we tend to view drug addicts as being bad, and we are less able to empathise with people who we define as bad. As we stereotype them as bad people, we in effect fail to understand or sympathise fully with their problems. Marlett shows the human angle, and from it we get a chance to understand and therefore relate better to such individuals. He brings up statistical evidence to show that a considerable proportion of relapses are due to interpersonal conflict, anxieties, and social pressure. The drugs seem to be the main self-help treatment which many addicts have available to help them cope with depressing experiences and negative feelings. It seems likely therefore that they would be less inclined to use drugs if they became better at managing negative feelings. Yes these guys are human after all and deserve some empathy!

Question 2: Does this research suggest that the kind of advice Bethune outlined is the best advice?

Task 4: To consider the importance of good attitudes[11]
Carl Rogers the founder of the counselling movement, believed that a major reason why counsellors are successful is because they develop certain key qualities[8]. These are:
* Having unconditional positive regard for people. This means you see the positive in them no matter what.
* Being genuine and not two-faced. This involves self-knowledge, so that you know how you are feeling, and can see when you are being two-faced.
* Being non-defensive when criticised.
* Being non- possessive so you do not demand people always live up to your demands and needs.
* Having respect for people - their feelings and values.

Task 5: Could you Use Counselling Techniques?
So if your son was angry and depressed about having acted foolishly, would you be able to use cognitive counselling techniques so as to help him to move on from discouraged and self-downing attitudes? One kind of problem that people tend to have is denial. Denial is created by our tendency to defend ourselves from the blows of life; we just fail to

recognise our contributions to problems. Strong angry feelings plus a denial tendency can make us wrongly attributes blame totally to other people for things going wrong. Denial also leads a person to be convinced that he is acting as constructively as possible despite there being evidence to the contrary. In this situation, counselling techniques may help:

* to get the client to consider if he does anything that is even a little wrong or unconstructive;
* to get the client to have more empathy for the person with whom he is angry;
* to get the client to write down the advantages and disadvantages of changing (a standard cognitive technique for the treatment of addiction);
* to get the client to make memo cards which remind him of the constructive ways he wants to think about things, and his own plans;
* to get a client to realise that if he goes out with a friend who is into drugs he will be far more likely to take drugs himself than if he went out with one of his non-drug friends;
* through explaining the problems of group influence, thus giving the client a clear rationale for working on his attitudes to different groups; and
* through looking at the thoughts he has when he fails to be assertive, thus helping the client to use self-argument (an RSA) so that he feels stronger in such situations (see Chapter 13 on assertiveness).

Hopefully you will have found that this chapter provides you with a flexible way of living more at ease with family problems while doing all you can to help family members to take stock and improve their lives. By reducing your depressive thinking and anger you can help troubled relatives. You won't see them as being the cause of your family sickness. Instead you will realise that the family sickness can be overcome. You just have to value the positive things about your own life. The more you get on with enjoying your own life the more you will have energy to help troubled family members. Why allow depression or shame to drain your energy? You and your family can grow and develop much better if you can embrace hope and happiness.

Chapter 16
You Can Even Cope with Big Problems such as Grief

Task 1: To see how problems are not always clear cut

Some problems are straightforward. For instance, your pop group breaks up. It's a clear-cut case of disappointment, hopes dashed, loss of friends, and the frustration of having to start all over again, building up contacts with bass players, drummers, etc.

On other occasions, though, problems can only be understood if you thoroughly investigate what's going on. You have to pinpoint:

* why exactly it is a problem;
* how you feel about it;
* how aspects of the problem link together; and
* how knock-on effects from other problems affect this one.

If you write up the problem on a mind map, you will see the connecting aspects more clearly.

Task 2: To consider how rational emotive behavioural therapy helps with understanding problems better

According to REBT we tend to plough into feelings. We get into deeper levels of feeling than we often need. For example, if a family member dies you will naturally be very sad, but often the sadness slips into depressed moods as well. There is a snowballing effect; you can end up feeling ashamed about looking sad and yet hardly realise the subtle changes taking place in your feelings.

It is almost as though you dived into a swimming pool but instead of managing to swim you went straight down to the bottom. At the bottom of this imaginary swimming pool people experience: depressing thoughts, strong feelings, black and white attitudes and rating of self as = 0

An exercise I use which helps with this ploughing into feelings problem is the sink and swim exercise. It is like diving into a pool. You write your thoughts and feelings on a diving diagram with arrows going down your page. Then you try to swim back up again by having calm, sensible thoughts to replace the sad, gloomy ones.

Sink and Swim Exercise

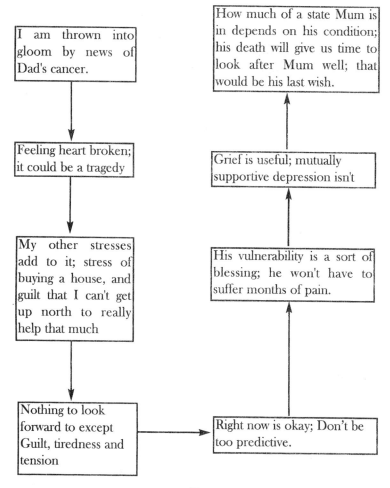

Task 3: To consider the usefulness of rational emotive imagery

Doing Rational Emotive Imagery (REI) is like doing a body workout. Every day you do something to develop your muscles or keep fit, but you also need to strengthen your mind. Like body workouts mind workouts help best when they are done again and again. With REI you are going to find out how to forcefully change your familiar thinking habits. When people get stuck with thinking in ways that are familiar to them they:

* fail to adapt;
* marry unsuitable partners;
* stay in depressing modes of thought.

How to do rational emotive imagery

Imagery is about imagining a situation fully. It draws you into the kinds of feelings you get when you are down. So let's try imagining a sad situation:

* You dumped your last girlfriend just two months ago.
* You've just become really attracted to a very pretty girl.
* You can at times feel sad, guilty and depressed about this.

So imagine the situation and get in touch with the feelings. You feel rotten about it, you feel sorry for her, etc. Now you have to use force in your mind and try to see things in a less extreme way. You can feel some guilt but you don't have to feel rotten. Why not? What kinds of sensible thoughts can you come up with? The 3 parts of Rational Emotive Imagery are:

1. Imagine a problem situation fully with all the associated feelings and thoughts.
2. Use force in your mind.
3. See the situation in a less extreme way.

Let's try another example:
* Your granny has died.
* You have been very sad.
* You now feel very self-conscious about feeling sad.

Now apply the three key aspects of REI listed above.
One final example will help you to appreciate the full range of uses of REI:
* You are aged 51.
* You are writing a book.
* You keep on having to re-write chunks of it.
* You are becoming a couch potato.
* You know you should be taking exercise.
* You are getting used to a comfortable life.

Apply REI to this situation.

Question 1:   How can you use rational emotive imagery for a problem in your life.

Task 4: To realise the importance of working on each problem thought

People often find that they have to investigate exactly what is on their minds in order to change thoroughly their negative attitudes. It can be useful to try to change each of the 'awful' thoughts in our minds.

It is important to remind you that by using REI you are able to work on each problem thought. For example, if you were experiencing the first problem we looked at in Task 3 above, namely you had dumped your girlfriend and you are now feeling guilty, then the main thought you have to work on is: 'I know that what I did was dreadful'.

Your best chance of changing this unpleasant thought is then to think: 'I can learn from this mistake. In the future I will have better values so that I care more about people I could hurt'.

Task 5: To use a variety of techniques for working on big problems

People need different kinds of exercises in order to work on big problems. There are several reasons for this. Firstly, big problems need to be chipped away at before their effects on our moods lift. Secondly, people are all different; some suit one kind of exercise, and others suit another. Different situations also suit different exercises. For example, a client may be suffering from self-damning. However, this self-critical mood may be caused by shame and/or guilt. Shame (with or without associated guilt) can be worked on by using an ABC form, but the guilt problem often needs an exercise like the one below before full resolution is achieved.

The guilt exercise

1. Write down several things that you feel you dislike about yourself and the way in which you handled a problem recently

2. Allow negative feelings and thoughts to drift into your mind concerning these.

3. Debate these but keep in mind self-acceptance slogans, such as 'The more I accept myself, the more other people will accept me.'

4. Finally, write a conclusion about what you now think, and what you intend to do from now on. You will feel slightly negative feelings bubbling up about parts of it, so you will need to write it again and again, up to five times, adding new important thoughts as you go, so that your conscious and unconscious minds fully accept things and move on.

Question 2: Try to catalogue all the kinds of exercises you have read about in this book so far. For example, there was the cognitive diary, the RSA, the self-counselling exercise, bibliotherapy, the additive empathy exercise.

Sometimes people come up with novel ways of doing self-help exercises. One young man who was miserable because a relationship had come to an end wrote a song called 'Stronger Fit Man'. This became something of a motto for him. Another student was upset about becoming very tall. He made up a play called 'Height' about a young child who had a different problem - he was too small. It was a very amusing play, and it helped the student to cultivate a sense of humour about life's problems.

Question 3:   Write a song or poem that is about a person having strength of character. Try to come up with something that fits your situation.

Question 4:   Try to catalogue 'your most uplifting songs of all time' and tell a close friend about your choices, or perform an amusing role-play that relates to your situation.

One very useful way of coping when in difficult situations is to have a set of memo cards. These can help you to keep calm but also to work out what you have to do to come through successfully.

Question 5:   Imagine you have to walk home at night through a rough area of town. Make up memo cards to help with coping in this situation.

Question 6:   Imagine you are a student teacher with a difficult class. How could having memo cards help?

Question 7:   Make up memo cards for a problem situation of your own.

Task 6: To focus your problem so you become aware of the effects of irrational beliefs

Irrational beliefs are attitudes that do you no good because:
* they are self-defeating;
* they merely drain your energy (see Chapter 11);
* they make you feel rotten, ashamed and hopeless; and
* they prevent you from developing your values (see Chapter 18 on managing transitions).

Question 8:   Draw your problem situation as if it were a forest. What sorts of things are happening in the drawing? Is it raining? Where are you? What are you doing? Who are the other people in the drawing? Now draw a wall in the centre of the forest. Often in life we feel we are banging our heads against brick walls and getting nowhere. In what ways does your situation give you the sore head and wall frustration? Can you find any negative beliefs that may be the cause of your frustration?

Rational emotive therapy teaches that we all have a tendency to suffer from a few powerful bad beliefs, as outlined by Ellis[12] which can be defined as irrational beliefs. These beliefs include:
* It is awful when things go badly for us.
* It is necessary to be approved of by almost everyone.
* People make us unhappy - we are helpless victims.
* I should be a success in all respects and very popular.
* People who do bad things are bad and wicked.
* People should behave reasonably at all times.
* We should be terribly worried about dangers and the awful consequences of being rejected.

Notice that this list of irrational beliefs is quite like the negative beliefs you worked on in Chapter 11.

Changing irrational beliefs
It is awful when things go badly for us

Challenge: When conditions seem undesirable try to view them philosophically. We get nowhere by making demands about life - our musts and shoulds. Hostility and the desire to have things easy merely stop us from working hard and patiently at making life better.

It is necessary to be approved of by almost everyone

Challenge: See approval as desirable but not necessary. Seriously consider people's criticisms of you without accepting their negative judgements of you.

People make us unhappy - we are helpless victims

Challenge: Realise that we make ourselves unhappy with our feelings and the propaganda that we tell ourselves. Our thoughts are not usually terribly clever - generally they are automatic and come from our rigid personalities. Therefore we would be wise to try to change our thoughts and feelings and get lots of practice in how to do this.

I should be a success in all respects and very popular

Challenge: Strongly desire success and work for it but do not believe that it makes you a more worthwhile person. Accept failure as undesirable but not awful - it has nothing to do with your worth as a human being.

People who do bad things are bad and wicked

Challenge: Get rid of the idea that you can define some people as bad and wicked. Fully accept human failings or you will be perfectionistic in the demands you make of yourself and others. While you try to learn from your mistakes and misdeeds, make allowances for the certain fact that in life we (and others) continue to make numerous errors and mistakes.

People should behave reasonably at all times

Challenge: Strongly desire to be treated reasonably but do not allow yourself to be drawn into having unrealistic standards. Your 'shoulds' just cause you needless frustration. It is as if you are trying to invent the laws of the universe and also insisting that other people keep to them.

We should be terribly worried about dangers and the awful consequences of being rejected

Challenge: The mind tends to awfulise and overstates the horrors and threats of not fitting in with other people. Look for your internal awfulising sentences and then weigh up accurately the real risks.

Action

Having thought about irrational beliefs, you may now feel able to apply the written exercise below to your problem. Notice that you have to try to identify your 'awfuls', your 'shoulds' and your rating statements below, then examine them using some of the questions provided.

First, describe a problem in column A (Activating event). Then go to column C and write down your feelings. (See diagram overpage).

Second, write down any awfuls in column B1, namely the irrational beliefs you have relating to the problem, followed by any associated 'shoulds', 'musts' and ratings in columns B2 and B3.

Another way of working on the effects of irrational beliefs is by understanding that in difficult situations we tend to get both rational and irrational thoughts. We could benefit from noting these in separate columns on an ABC form. The reason why this is useful is because rational and irrational thoughts tend to be tied up together like strands of a rope. You only recognise that you have both kinds of thoughts by unpicking the rope strands. Then when you see clearly both the rational and irrational thoughts you can work on strengthening the rational and disputing the irrational.

A: The Problem	
	Questions
B1: Awfuls and Irrational Beliefs	Can these awfuls be reinterpreted in any way?
B2: 'Shoulds' and 'Musts'	Is my 'should' causing my angry 'awful' statements? Is my 'must' making me rate my weakness and myself as totally unacceptable?
B3: Ratings	
C: Feelings	Can I still be happy despite this?
D: New Feelings	

A: Activating Event	B1: Rational Beliefs	B2: Irrational beliefs	C: Feelings

Points to remember

* Rational thoughts are about preferences not 'got to's' or 'shoulds' or 'musts'.
* Rational thoughts are calm and logical.
* Rational thoughts do not cause you to act self-defeatingly.
* Rational thoughts are linked to being ethical.

Task 7: To know which therapy to use

This chapter has really reconsidered the variety of techniques that have been explored earlier in the book. Some of these techniques can be seen as being behaviourist, for example making up memo cards to help cope with fear.

Question 9:   Look back at Chapter 9 on being a better sportsperson. Find once again what it says about behaviourism. Why is the memo card technique an example of behaviourism?

Let's recall that the two main therapies on which this book focuses are called cognitive behavioural therapy and rational emotive behavioural therapy (REBT). The cognitive approach leans more towards the idea of using debate to change mistaken assumptions. The rational emotive approach focuses more on changing the awfuls. At an emotional level, awfuls tend to be seen as 100% bad. That means that the kinds of errors you get in the logic of awful thoughts lead them to become too definite, too definitional. Therefore, the focus of rational emotive approach is to try to help people to reconsider just how awful things are. Look back at the part of this chapter dealing with irrational beliefs. These beliefs are examples of typical awfulising statements, so these exercises clearly are derived from REBT.

This chapter has clearly featured exercises that come from REBT because, instead of finding assumptions to reinterpret, you are just struggling to dispute and debate the extreme thoughts as best you can. Notice that the rational emotive approach is sometimes fairly similar to cognitive behavioural therapy so you do not really have to worry about getting them mixed up.

Chapter 17
Do You Need Goals?

Task 1: To consider how working on goals fits into the counselling approach

We have seen how the exploration of feelings and negative thoughts is the central strategy for treating depression. However, working on feeling states and challenging negative thoughts seem to be tasks that bear no relationship to having goals. Yet where would we be without goals in life? Without goals there would be no room for ambition, self-improvement and moving forward in our lives. Clearly we need to find ways of considering goals along with our feelings about these goals. In other words, we need to fit goals into our counselling model and develop skilled techniques for working on both goals and feelings. Perhaps at this point it is useful to create a model showing how goals-directed work fits into the counselling process.

Counselling Process

↓

Exploration Stage
Empathy and open-ended questions help with wide exploration of problems.

↓

Concreteness Search Stage
Mind maps, cognitive diaries and ABC forms help with concrete understanding of problems.

↓

Challenge Stage
Debating techniques such as RSA forms help but also the consideration of goals helps to move people forward by overcoming problems and regaining hope.

Task 2: To consider how to work on goal-related problems

Sometimes when exploring a client's problems, I notice that the client seems most concerned about coming through a difficult time that he/she expects to have in the near future. When that happens, I find that a technique called forcefield analysis helps me to get insights into just why the client is fearful of the impending changes.

Are there areas in your life where you would like to be more effective, for example, managing your health or developing career aims or business skills? Forcefield analysis is the technique to consider:

1. Restraining factors: How do you get stuck and prevented from acting effectively. What negative feelings block your progress? Do your attitudes or values prevent you from adapting?

2. Facilitating factors: This involves listing the good things about you, such as attitudes, skills and knowledge, and the support you have from other people, which can help you to become more effective in the pursuit of your goal.

Once you have listed the restraining factors and the facilitating factors (you can show them on a snakes and ladders diagram if you like) then you have to write an action plan, divided into two parts:

1. How I reduce my restraining factors.
2. How I increase my facilitating factors.

Finally, try to see how you are awfulising about making the necessary changes. List your awfulising thoughts and then try to change them. If you look back at the previous chapter on irrational beliefs, you may be fully aware of the ways we tend to awfulise and the more rational ideas we can have which help us to go forward with more positive attitudes.

See on the next page an example of a forcefield analysis form:

Forcefield Analysis	
My restraining factors:	My facilitating factors:
1. _____	1. _____
2. _____	2. _____
3. _____	3. _____
4. _____	4. _____

Action Plan

To reduce my restraining factors:

1. _____
2. _____
3. _____

To increase my facilitating factors:

1. _____
2. _____
3. _____

Awfulising thoughts:	Improved thoughts:
1. _____	1. _____
2. _____	2. _____
3. _____	3. _____
4. _____	4. _____

Task 3: To work on choices and the feelings we have about these choices

Sometimes when we have a difficult choice to make a simple balance sheet with pro and con columns can help us to consider our attitudes to each choice. Our feelings about each choice can be addressed if we consider what mark out of ten to give each of the points in the balance sheet. Then the choice becomes easier. You simply add up all the marks for the choice and then add up all the marks against it. However, we sometimes find that a lot of choices and issues need to be addressed so that we can overhaul our lives in a wide-ranging way. This is when you need the more complicated Values Analysis Sheet which I have outlined on the next page.

Value Analysis Sheet			
Different choices			
Awfulising about each choice			
Ethics concerning the choices			
What's in it for others?			
What's in it for me?			
What's not in it for me?			
Counter the awfulising			
Final rating of each choice.			

Hopefully you have seen how to integrate goal setting into the counselling process. The techniques we have considered also help you to find room for the consideration of your feelings within goal setting.

In the next chapter on transitions, you will find that action plans can be dealt with from a counselling angle and have several specific purposes.

This chapter has also helped you to reconsider the whole counselling approach as a model involving exploration of problems, concreteness search and challenge. This helps you to catalogue the process and skills more clearly, and therefore makes your use of self-counselling more strategic.

Chapter 18
Strategies for Coping with Transitions

Task 1: To consider what a transition is

A transition may be viewed as a long time of change in your life. Moreover, it is a time of frustration and disappointment when things seem to be moving forward too slowly. People feel puzzled about how they will get through their long tunnel. Sometimes you go one step forward and two back. Sometimes there is sadness because the difficult transition perhaps begins as a result of a painful life experience.

People often think that the teenage years or middle age can become difficult times of transition. Not everyone moves smoothly through the life tasks that people face during these stages of life. However, you can suffer from a transition at any time in your life. The main way you would know if you were experiencing a Transition is probably through your feelings. You just know that the slowness of change and the difficulties of the journey are affecting your moods. The difficulties perhaps also make you clumsy so that once in a negative mood you start behaving somewhat unpredictably, not quite sure why you feel uneasy and not quite understanding why you can't act sensibly in this condition.

Task 2: To consider how you can accept the tunnel

When going through a transition it seems like a long frustrating tunnel. The light at the end of it, turns out to be an on-coming train. However, it is no good getting terribly frustrated in this tunnel. You must get to like the tunnel, and be patient in it. For example, you might need to get really involved in some activity that in time can become the stepping stones that take you through your transition. Whether the essential activity is a weight-watchers organisation, a church, or an educational establishment, really give it your full concentration and interest. Let's take another example. Imagine you are a recovering drug addict. Your problem is that you don't have all the money you need right now to pay the bills. Get your binoculars out and just focus on the most essential bill. Consider how far you can negotiate on the rest. In other words deal with an aspect of the problem and quit worrying about the rest. In a transition you have to focus on essentials, but also keep to workable and sensible goals.

Example

A parent I knew was worried about the possibility that he would not be able to see his children again. His wife talked about taking them abroad some time in the future and separating from him. His marriage seemed to hang in the balance, and he could lose everything. He talked about his affection for them and concern about their schoolwork. I helped him to create hypnotherapy tapes that helped him to work on the 'I can't stand it' mood. In the tapes he would use some of the progressive relaxation techniques that we studied in Chapter 12. He would add visualisation to the relaxing instructions. For example, he visualised a burning candle, then the imagery of going down flumes into a deep warm swimming pool. Then the image of flowing down a smooth river and ending up floating gently along a very still canal was added. Then the following suggestions were put forcefully on to the tape.

"Sometimes in life we can't guarantee that our love will last forever. However we can pass on our 'ISM'. Your own personal 'ISM', whether it is socialism, liberalism, conservatism or religion, can still be passed on. You will have left it, carefully thought out, like a rich tapestry that your children can explore for themselves. Your 'ISM' is a love you have for the whole world. It is a giving love, one that transcends personal life and ego. In it we live beyond the present and in spite of the weight we carry from the past. As you keep your nerve and think beyond the negative prospects, so you gain more power to influence the course of your family's lives."

Task 3: To consider exactly how the shoes pinch

Many people don't realise how difficult it is to work out exactly what has been going wrong when things in our lives turn out badly. This problem may become more obvious if we think for a moment about our earlier clients William and his wife Mary, and how they have been having problems with their small son. William and Mary don't really seem to know why things go so badly wrong, but we can perhaps suggest some possible causes of their general malaise. Look back at Chapter 3 on self-counselling techniques. and then try to complete the diagnostic sheet below using your own ideas about the issues you think they need to work on during their time in counselling.

Counselling Diagnostic Sheet for William and Mary
Issues that may need to be worked on are:
* _____
* _____
* _____
* _____
* _____

William's wife Mary has finally agreed to come for counselling. Early on in the counselling, she tells her counsellor about how a general insecure mood keeps her in a depressive malaise, and prevents her having quality time with her son. The counsellor teaches her to use a 'de-buting' form which helps her to consider her negative reactions while also trying to counter them. The exercise involves writing a negative thought at the top left-hand of the page then trying to counteract it with an arrow connecting to the new thought on the right. An arrow then to the left to another negative thought and you must try to counteract it again. See the example below, showing how Mary wants to get over her depressed way of thinking, so that she can really enjoy taking her son out to the museum, the play park, etc. Below is her 'de-but-ing' diagram.

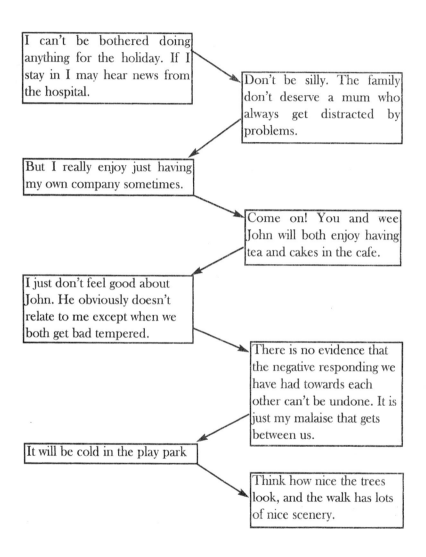

I can't be bothered doing anything for the holiday. If I stay in I may hear news from the hospital.

Don't be silly. The family don't deserve a mum who always get distracted by problems.

But I really enjoy just having my own company sometimes.

Come on! You and wee John will both enjoy having tea and cakes in the cafe.

I just don't feel good about John. He obviously doesn't relate to me except when we both get bad tempered.

There is no evidence that the negative responding we have had towards each other can't be undone. It is just my malaise that gets between us.

It will be cold in the play park

Think how nice the trees look, and the walk has lots of nice scenery.

Task 4 : To work on perfectionism

Anne has been seeing a therapist because of problems with dieting excessively. She may be anorexic. She first dieted two years ago and felt very pleased with the way her success in shedding weight led to increased popularity. Now whenever she comes to eat food she feels worry and guilt about the effects of overeating. She knows that if she doesn't keep strict control she will just binge and then feel really bad about it later. Her therapist finds that she has some very black and white thoughts relating to the whole area of food and relationships. These thoughts are:

* If I eat a bar of chocolate it will go straight onto my waistline.
* Fat is bad for your health; it's disgusting to eat fatty things.
* You need a relationship with the opposite sex to be happy; being on your own is a lonely existence.
* You can only be attractive if you are thin.
* If I eat some chocolate I will lose control and binge.

The therapist questioned her black and white conclusions very gently. His aim was just to let her see that these views were just beliefs (or hypotheses) not actually facts. Then he set her an action plan which involved her doing several tasks.

GLOSSARY: Action Plans

An action plan can usefully be introduced during a counselling interview to help a client to:
* manage a crisis;
* take a series of steps that will improve things;
* challenge their beliefs by helping them to get evidence that disproves their negative and pessimistic conclusions.

For example, James (an ME sufferer) was helped to take up a favourite sport once again. This led to an improvement in his fitness and lifted his pessimistic view that he was too tired to function adequately.

Anne's action plan involved getting her firstly to eat a small amount of food in front of the therapist and see if in fact she could get control over the desire to eat more and the anxieties that eating usually caused.

115

Secondly, she was asked to take up an interesting hobby that did not involve contact with the opposite sex and see if it was possible to enjoy herself without being in a relationship, and without being a perfect shape.

Question: How were Anne's beliefs a recipe for making her perfectionistic?

In a transition you face new life events. The skills you have learned and which helped you to cope well in the past perhaps no longer seem effective in dealing with the new experience. So it is important to give up the perfectionistic view that you should always be a success, you should never need help, and you should not have to talk about your feelings.

When going through a transition you should perhaps try not to carry unnecessary baggage. Angry memories and old resentments don't help you to walk your tightrope. The tightrope of your life, though, still has to be walked. In the next chapter I will return to this theme and consider how far the influence of the Ancient Greek philosophers - the Stoics - have helped people in the past to live their lives bravely and ethically. Indeed, can religion and philosophy help us to cope better with depression, and also with the long transitions that we all have to face at some time or other?

Chapter 19
Help from Ancient Philosophy
and Rational Emotive Therapy

Staring down at me from a staff-room noticeboard was an insightful placard. It read: 'We've discovered what causes mental distress - life'. The clever devils, I thought. There is no answer to that. It's exactly what you're up against when you try to do a spot of counselling. Your son is down because his career life and love life have both nose-dived. No cunning rationalisations will do. Cause of mental distress? Life! A friend tells you he is depressed because he has been made redundant and has separated from his wife all at one blow. Problems seem to come in waves, never singly, but from all angles. You soon find yourself surrounded by the casualties of life.

The words of Rudyard Kipling in his famous poem 'If' seemed to spring to mind as I listened sympathetically to my son's career and love-life woes.[13]

'If you can keep your head when all about you are losing theirs ...
If you can trust yourself when all men doubt you ...
If you can wait and not be tired by waiting ...'[10]

Suddenly I saw how to apply them to his problem. The solution was right in front of my eyes - his 18th birthday card showing a man walking on a sandy beach.

'Okay', I said, grasping the nettle heroically. 'Compare your life for a minute to that man walking in the sand. Possibly he's just a little lost and is now anxious to find his way back to his hotel. Now he probably has to make some choices of routes so he finds the quickest way back. But the good news is that he only has a couple of options to try out before he finds his way and in the meantime he can enjoy the scenery and the journey. Now is there any way that applies to you?'

I could see that my son was trying hard to review his situation in this very positive light. So, after some further rumination I felt that it was safe to share with him the words of Kipling's 'If'. The inspiration of that father - son pep talk seems to have paid off because months later he was still reminding me of how much he had seen into the meanings of that walk in the sand.

'How do you cope when your chances of happiness seem to be less than 40%?' my redundant friend had asked me. To answer his question I gave him a history lesson about Epictetus, a slave who lived in Ancient Rome. He must have known all about 'the life stinks' problem - after all he was a slave. Well Epictetus stayed calm, got educated and contributed to the development of Stoic philosophy and then to Roman law. His thinking about being stoical was so important that it influenced a whole range of future writers from Shakespeare to Kipling and, in the present day, therapists such as Ellis.

Quite simply, these Stoic philosophers knew the importance of positive thinking. You just have to refuse to be negative. After all, things could be worse. This is what one Stoic philosopher wrote:

'Let's say you think money is a good thing: then you will be tortured by poverty and - what is worse - an unreal poverty. However rich you are, you will find someone richer and so regard yourself as so much the poorer.
You are so gripped by ambition that if you aren't first you'll think you're last. Or perhaps you think death is the worst thing of all: but the only thing bad about death is what comes before it - fear' [11]

The Stoics' positive thinking abilities were also greatly helped by their attachment to kindness and values. These attributes were inspiring to such men.

'"The power there is in an ideal to bring about its own reality was exemplified many a time in these days of Rome. In the city where Tacitus and Juvenal saw public exhibitions of unnamable

vice, the Stoics lived lives of austere purity...

In an age of cruelty, widespread as it never was to be again, the Stoics declared the cruel man to be possessed by 'a dreadful disease of the mind'...

They were alone too, in teaching that a slave was to be treated as a human being. This insistence was the logical result of their belief in 'the true light, which lighteth every man that cometh into the world'...

The principle which became fundamental in Roman law, that all men are by nature equal, was derived, the historians agree, from the Stoics, and if Stoicism had no other claim to admiration, that alone would set it high amoung the great beneficent activities of the world." (Hamilton, The Roman Way 148-9). [12]

There are many forms of positive thinking, and various religions also help with the development of values.

In modern times, REBT has come the closest to copying Stoic ways of thinking. In rational emotive therapy, work is done to get people to give up their mistaken attitudes. They have to change their irrational beliefs (see Chapter 16 for some examples).

How about a few more Stoical words from Kipling's poem 'If',

> *'If you can make one heap of all your winnings*
> *And risk it on one turn of pitch-and-toss*
> *And lose, and start again at your beginnings*
> *And never breathe a word about your loss ...*
> *If you can fill the unforgiving minute*
> *With sixty seconds' worth of distance run,*
> *Yours is the Earth and everything that's in it,*
> *And - which is more - you'll be a Man my son.'*

Chapter 20
Has Stoicism always been in the Culture?

Stoicism did not survive as a cultural force after the decline of Rome, but the image of men being 'stoical' - able to put up with difficulties and thereby being stoical, strengthening their characters - did. Wherever Latin was read, this image of Romans, in the great days of their empire, lived on.

Indeed, the image of Roman greatness informed the centuries-old idealism of chivalry. Born in the legends of King Arthur and his knights the idea that knights had a huge duty to their society and to rescuing damsels in distress became the childhood stories that children right through the middle ages were brought up on.

In Scotland, the heroic images of clan chiefs, pipers, Highland games and clan traditions also kept a chivalrous sentiment alive. Our greatest hero, Robert and Bruce, was inspired by the concepts of chivalry and Christianity. Somehow his inspiration helped him through the bleak times of his life, when he lost his wife and brothers. Our traditional sense that it was good for children to know about these things bears a certain similarity to Stoicism - reading about heroes of the past gives a stoical 'metal' to our personalities.

However, it is not quite sufficient for society to have only a vague sense of stoicism. We need at least an awareness of how Stoicism is a real inspiration. Nowadays, the rational emotive and cognitive treatments for depression help us to appreciate the importance of being rational and how we can once again reconsider the value of the original ideas of the Stoic philosophers.

This book has tried to show that the thought processes and arguments of the Stoics can help people to cope with problems and compete better in the many theatres of life. In our daily battles with fitness, health, stress, depression and the elements, we need the patience and optimism that our ancestors often showed. Then, as we calmly go through the transitions of our lives 'the wheel will turn for us. If stoicism has been preserved through our history and through our heroic traditions, then is religion also good for us and part of the heroic tradition?

In Scotland, our earliest stories of religious people have been of the wandering holy men. Saint Columba is one example. The images of these early saints have been of men who were kind and dedicated to converting the tribes to Christianity. The images of our more recent preachers have been more controversial and less clearly benign. However, Christianity has occasionally found the same calibre of inspiring men who did indeed influence their communities. Donald Sage was one such person - a minister in the Highlands of Scotland in the early nineteenth century. He wrote his life story in his book Memorabilia Domestica[13]. As a youngster he believed that God was an angry being. Some of the time he didn't allow himself to smile or joke for fear of God's wrath. Then he would get fed up with this restricted way of life and just go out and enjoy himself; he would rebel a bit and have a good time. However, his fear of God would eventually prey on his mind and he would return once again to the more solemn approach to life. Suddenly, one day, an idea came to his mind, 'salvation is not of debt but of grace'. In other words, God is just offering us a relationship, not asking us to keep paying debts for our past misbehaviour. He is not asking us to be perfect. Once Sage had successfully personified God as a loving figure, he was able to get into a Christian relationship with him. He went on to become a very successful minister.

Task 1: To Investigate the modern influences of Christianity

Modern evangelists seem to have been successful mainly when they have helped people to consider how the religious way is better than the 'worldy' way of living. Various famous pop stars for example have stated that guilt about drug taking and having casual sex has made them look again at religion as a better and more sensible way of life. Quite often evangelists have succeeded when they have clearly focussed on examples of things people do which are not honest. University Christian groups, may spend time discussing topics such as CD theft. This refers to the common modern tendency for people to download music from the internet and in effect deprive the musicians of payment for their work. Such discussions have a habit of turning into earnest analysis of whether masturbation could ever be justified, or whether taping friend's C.D.'s constitutes theft. Not surprisingly some students who embark on the religious path find that the perfectionistic demands it entails can become too depressing. Smashing their pirated CD's may do them no harm, but months of guilt-ridden anxiety about the human condition can mess their heads. Does religious thinking have to be too fanatical?

In Christian evangelical writing there is still a big tendency to focus on sin. However writers such as Ryrie and Hodge have shown that Saint Paul was sympathetic to Christians who continued to have problems with sin. Paul called them 'babes in Christ'. (See Ryrie 'So Great a Salvation') Is modern Christianity too perfectionistic?

Can religion be an effective force within a cognitive behavioural model of what is therapeutic for modern people? In so far as some preachers and some churches have managed to help individuals to feel close to God, it is perhaps a force for good. Given that religion sees all men as sinful, then you do not rate as any worse than the next man. You are not any more cut off from your God than the next man. Most religions suggest that a belief in God and a turning away from immorality can help any of us - no matter what sins you may have committed in the past. And so a key therapeutic idea can still be seen as valid. People can do bad things without being 'bad' in a total sense. We can do stupid things without being stupid. The logic of this argument has been central to helping people to get over their profound discouragement, as we have seen in previous chapters. No doubt the brief investigation of modern religion above may suggest to you positives and negatives about religion. No doubt it would be good if we all had some idea of morality; being moral can help us to keep out of trouble and prevent us being self-defeating in the way we live our lives. However, being fanatical can prevent us living in a realistic way; we can expect too much of ourselves and of other people. Some people may feel that being moral is good for you but living by just 'ten commandments' is both constricting and also offers only a narrow range moral guidance. For some people their concepts of morality may be better developed through the study of philosophy or of science. The negative images of Christianity from our past may convince some people that Christianity is too insensitive, and churches too narrow in their condemnation of certain kinds of immoral behaviour. After all, since the Enlightenment of the eighteenth century, philosophy and science have been features of our heroic tradition. In Scotland great figures like Robert Owen, the Welsh owner of New Lanark cotton factory and David Hume, the philosopher, have been inspiring figures of the Enlightenment. We have had great socialist writers, feminists, liberals and conservatives who have contributed to our heroic heritage.

Task 2: To investigate the value of philospohy [21]

I can hear you ask, 'What is philosophy?' so let me quote that great populiser of the subject, Bryan Magee from his book 'The Story of Philosophy':[19] "Philosophy begins when human beings start trying to understand the world not through religion or by accepting authority but through the use of reason."

Throughout history the great writers of philosophy have left their ideas for us to debate. Socrates, one of the early Greek writers, believed that the ideas of justice should be questioned - we should discuss the fairness of society and thereby make it better. Aristotle, another of the Greek writers, was seen as a voice of moderation, helping us to avoid some of the worst effects of fanaticism. Magee's favourite modern philosophers have been Arthur Schopenhaur, who brought Buddhist ideas into Western thought, and Immanuel Kant, whose ideas of 'the moral imperative' seem to derive more from traditional religion.

However, to be a stoical person one has to identify with the heroic aspects of culture in a broad sense. The cognitive psychotherapies, with their exercises for changing negative thoughts and feelings, also seem to belong to our heroic tradition. For those of us who find the ideas of therapy to be inspiring, the work on mental errors, emotional reasoning and black and white thinking tendencies becomes an ongoing part of one's life. Then, like the salmon, we swim up-river, like the dog we have our day, like the tightrope walker we calmly face our fearful journey. Our best chance of lasting happiness comes from learning how to transcend difficulties; we escape from our learned helplessness into learned hopefulness.

Some final thoughts

This book has been inspired by Carl Rogers, who developed the concept of counselling in the 1950s. The main influence, though, has been Albert Ellis, the key writer on rational emotive behavioural therapy. Also, the influence of cognitive behavioural therapy theorists, such as David Burns, has been important. It would be nice if such complex ideas could be defined very simply as it would help all our readers to demystify the cognitive therapies. The concept of counselling can be summed up in a reasonably straightforward way. The idea we examined in the first chapter is that we can benefit from just reflecting on feelings. By doing this, we sense our feelings more authentically and explore their nature and associated thoughts. It is like peeling off layers of an onion; we get to be more in touch with all the feelings and more clearly sense how the shoe hurts. Cognitive theory is also reasonably easy to grasp. Cognitive behavioural therapists believe that underlying our negative feelings we tend to have assumptions, which can be checked out. Are we maximising the meaning of criticisms, making over-generalised statements, or mind reading and expecting disapproval? Rational emotive behavioural therapy is the therapy that seems the hardest to define. The ideas are certainly valid - that we have negative ratings which underlie our depressed feelings. These negative ratings are our 'awfuls', our 'shoulds' and our 'musts'.

If you look back at my sink and swim exercise in Chapter 16, you will see that the exercise helped me to escape from my preoccupation with seeing the bereavement situation as totally awful. Similarly, in Chapter 15, Bethune's advice that it is possible for you to get on with your life even though you have a difficult relative seems to help us to change perspective and escape from the negative definition of the problem situation. Things don't have to be totally awful. And in the final chapter we noted how Robert the Bruce's attachment to chivalry helped him to get some resolution of the depressing blows that devastated his family life. Perhaps the simplest definition, therefore, of rational emotive behavioural theory is that it shows us how to wrestle with the 'awfuls' in our lives and potentially find some way to change negative perspectives.

Simple definitions are useful; by getting the sense of things 'in a nutshell' we become more able to employ the ideas in our strategies of coping with life. I hope you have found that this book has achieved for you the aim I had at conception, that it would help you to demystify the cognitive therapies and thereby help you to beat depression with self-help techniques. Best of luck with your journey.

Appendix 1
Counselling Techniques

Below I have presented a summary of the main techniques used in Counselling.

DOOR OPENER: This is when you show you recognize the nature of the problem the client is trying to outline and ask him (or her) to tell you more about it.

EMPATHY: The technique of understanding feelings is called EMPATHY. To use it fully try to say to yourself 'you feel... because of... and the effect is...' The technique has two parts to it. There is

REFLECTION OF CONTENT: This is when the Counsellor focuses on what the Client has been saying and briefly summarises it.

REFLECTION OF FEELING: This involves using feeling words to help the client to be aware of his reactions.

OPEN ENDED QUESTIONS: There are closed questions and open ended questions in Counselling. A closed question asks for a fact, like 'What is your job? An open question asks about an aspect of a situation. For example you could ask a client 'How are things going for you at work right now?

A MINIMAL ENCOURAGER: Can be a very useful question technique. . A minimum encourager is like asking a question. You take a key word or phrase the Client has used and put it back to the client in a questioning way.

PARAPHRASES: Paraphrases are brief summaries which reflect the client's thinking. Paraphrases correctly mirror the sad conclusions which the client seems to be making. This attending to the client's extreme thoughts is every bit as important as attending to his feelings.

CONCRETENESS SEARCH: Concreteness search is:
* when you try to understand problems more concretely
* look for specific negative thoughts as in a Cognitive Thoughts Diary
* consider which aspects of problems need to worked on first.

A.B.C. FORMS OR COGNITIVE DIARIES: An A.B.C. form is very useful for the CONCRETENESS SEARCH stage of Self Counselling. This is because it helps one to work out thoughts and feelings. The negative feelings will correspond to negative thoughts, so if you locate a strong feeling you can look for a strong thought which relates to it.

GIVING A RATIONALE: This is when a Counsellor gives an explanation of why he is about to use a technique or why he is interested in a certain aspect of a problem. The explanation helps both Counsellor and Client to focus on the work which is about to be done.

CHALLENGE: Challenge involves:
* Using PARAPHRASES to focus on the precise nature of the negative thoughts.
*Then asking a key question which could make the client think about whether the negative thought is correct or incorrect.
* You can also invite the client to think out better ways of looking at the situation in a Cognitive diary or an A.B.C. form or in some other self help form.

CHAINING: Chaining is so called because by asking the question why repeatedly you go down a chain until you get to the real answer. For example Counsellor asks a client; 'Why would it be so awful if your daughter burst into tears? The response was; 'It would make me feel like a bad mother.' The Counsellor then enquired, 'Why would it be awful to have this feeling of being a bad mother?' The response was because my husband used to tell the kids that mummy's a bad mother.

The day he left us two years ago he said to Janet, "Make sure mummy behaves well." His attitude has put a huge strain on my relationship with the children." So what did that make you feel about yourself? "I felt more like the naughty daughter than the parent of this family."

ADDITIVE EMPATHY: Additive Empathy is when a Counsellor tries to see the implications of what the client has been telling him. So the Counsellor:
* Shows a logical implication of how a client feels
* Considers the general picture and draws the client's attention to overlooked aspects.
* Compares different themes to help a client make new insights.

ACTION PLANS: An action plan can usefully be introduced during a Counselling interview to help
* A client to manage a Crisis
* To help the client take a series of steps which will improve things
* To help challenge a Client's beliefs by helping him get evidence, which disproves his negative and pessimistic conclusions.

Appendix 2
Cognitive Therapy -
Mental Errors - Fully Explored

Below I present a full glossary of the mental errors, which have been described by Cognitive Therapists, along with their meanings.

ALL OR NOTHING THINKING: This is when we see ourselves as either wonderful or worthless. For example we tell ourselves 'if I am not on top I am a flop'. Extreme 'all or nothing' thoughts then affect our self esteem.

BLACK AND WHITE THINKING: This is when we see things in a judgemental ways. We see ourselves or other people as either being very good or very bad, very wise or very stupid. For this reason our moral judgements can be too simplistic or too extreme. We also expect other people to adopt the same heavily critical or derogatory view of us, as we perhaps tend to have of them.

OVER-GENERALISING: this makes us tend to expect bad luck because of one bad experience. Or perhaps you notice that a person behaved badly on two occasions and from this you assume that he tends to misbehave all the time. The tendency people have to make over-generalisations causes them to be pessimistic. They sense that in life you always get bad luck. One bad experience proves you can't trust luck, other people, or life.

MENTAL FILTER: This is when you seize a negative aspect of a situation and dwell on it. It is as if you are looking at a part of the skyline, through binoculars, and you believe that you are able to see the entire skyline. So in effect you are focusing on one aspect of a problem, and you become unable to look more widely at the full picture.

PERSONALISATION: This kind of thinking leads us into self -critical attitudes .It focuses on the blame that could be landed on oneself. It's as if one sees oneself as the centre of the Universe. We are responsible for something going badly wrong. We forget that other people and even world events share responsibility. This thinking error causes us to be obsessed with SHOULDS and MUSTS. 'I should have done better' 'I must do well in every thing I try'. These shoulds and musts then promote guilt, shame, or defensiveness, and sometimes even DENIAL. Denial is caused when deep down we feel that if we behaved badly it would be truly awful- so we prefer to stick with trying to prove 'our own case' instead of looking open- mindedly at the unpalatable facts. We even forget about a bad action, so that it is blotted out from memory.

MAXIMISE THE MEANING: This is when we listen to a criticism and over-state its meaning. We then tend to think that they meant to be really hurtful, and that the criticism is unbearably heavy. We do all these negative things, instead of doing an obvious reflective thinking task- which is to reconsider the criticism in its' precise and minimal terms.

JUMPING TO CONCLUSIONS: You make assumptions (this is termed 'fortune telling' if the assumptions are about the future) and you draw conclusions from non-verbal evidence (termed 'mind reading') or from simplistic reasoning.

MIND READING: This is when we assume we know what people are thinking of us despite the lack of evidence. We just know that people are having a negative reaction to us. For this reason we don't do reality checking or considering the possibilities fully. 'Does that glare I got from my boss suggest he has taken a real dislike to me or is it just that I caught him in a moment of frustration?'

MAGNIFYING: is a common cause of anxiety. This is when we exaggerate the extent of a problem. We may overstate the extent to which the boss has taken a dislike to us. We may overstate the way one imperfection (e.g. spots on one's face) could make us unattractive. When magnifying is linked with fear it makes us focus only on the negative thoughts and negative sensations aroused by our fears.

CATASTROPHIZING: This is when we expect disaster to strike. We even fantasise about it happening and ask ourselves questions like 'What if the worst happened?' We torture ourselves by allowing such thoughts to go round and round in our heads. The negative images we get about fearful events (though fleeting) exert great power because they link in with our negative 'catastrophising' logic.

Further Reading

Beck Aaron T., Cognitive Therapy and the Emotional Disorders. Penguin, London, 1991

Bethune Helen. Off The Hook - Coping With Addiction. Methuen. London 1985

Burns David. Feeling Good : The New Mood Therapy. Avon Books. New York 1999.

Culley Sue. Integrative Counselling Skills in Action sage London 1991

Dryden Windy. Rational Emotive Counselling In Action. Sage, London 1999.

Ellis Albert. The Practice of Rational Emotive Behaviour Therapy, New York, Springer 1997

Ellis Albert & Harper, R.A. A New Guide To Rational Living. Atlantic Books. Henley on Thames 1961

Ellis Albert & Grieger Russell. A Handbook Of Rational Emotive Therapy. Springer London 1986.

Hawton Keith. Salkovskis Paul M. Kirk Joan. Clark David M. Cognitive Behavioural Therapy for Psychiatric Problems A Practical Guide Oxford University Press1989

McKay Matthew, Davis Martha, Fanning Patrick, Thoughts and Feelings Taking Control of Your Moods and Your Life, New Harbinger Publications, Oakland 1998

Mearns Dave. Thorne Brian. Person Centred Counselling in Action Sage London 1991

Munro Anne. Manthei Bob. Small John. Counselling the Skills of Problem Solving. Routledge. London 1989

Nelson-Jones Richard. Practical Counselling Skills Holt Rinehart & Winston. London 1983

Scott Jan. Williams J.Mark G. Beck Aaron T. Cognitive Therapy in Clinical Practice. Routledge. London 1989.

References

1. Rogers, Carl, Client Centred Therapy: its Current Practice, Implications and Theory, Constable & Robinson, London 2003

2. Ellis, Albert A New Guide to Rational Living, Atlantic Books, Henley on Thames, 1961

3. Gottman, John, Why Marriages Succeed or Fail: And How You Can Make Yours Last, Bloomsbury, London,1998, page 150

4. Ellis Albert The Practice of Rational Emotive Behaviour Therapy, New York, Springer 1997

5. McKay, Matthew, Davis, Martha, Fanning, Patrick, Thoughts and Feelings Taking Control of Your Moods and Your Life, New Harbinger Publications, Oakland 1998

6. Bethune, Helen, Off the Hook: Coping With Addiction, Methuen, London, 1985, page 67

7. Marlatt quated in Scott, Jan, Williams, J.Mark G. Beck, Aaron T. Cognitive Therapy in Clinical Practice an Illustrative Casebook Routledge, London 1989

8. Rogers, Carl, op cit

9. Ellis, Albert op cit

10. Kipling, Rudyard, 'If' Rewards and Fairies House of Stratus 2001

11. Nicholls, Roger and McLeish, Kenneth, Through Roman Eyes; Roman Civilization in the Words of Roman Writers, Cambridge University Press, Cambridge, 1976, page 17

12. Hamilton Edith, The Roman Way, W. w. Norton. New York, 1985

13. Sage, Donald, Memorabilia; Parish Life in the North of Scotland, Albyn, 1976

14. Magee, Bryan, The Story Of Philosophy, Dorling Kindersley, London 2001

Index